# 365

## DAYS OF
## PRAYER
## FOR

# MEN

**BroadStreet**
PUBLISHING

BroadStreet Publishing Group LLC
Savage, Minnesota, USA
Broadstreetpublishing.com

# 365 Days of Prayer for Men

© 2020 BroadStreet Publishing

978-1-4245-6461-3
978-1-4245-6096-7 (ebook)

Prayers composed by D. E. Gregory.

Design by Chris Garborg | garborgdesign.com
Edited by Michelle Winger | literallyprecise.com

Printed in China.

22 23 24 25 26  5 4 3 2 1

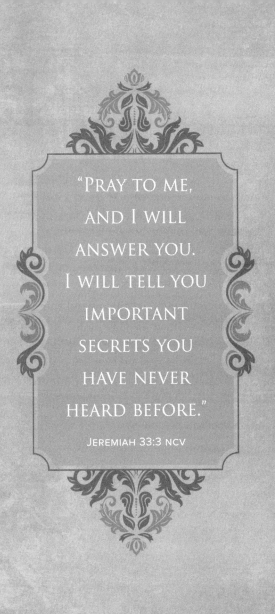

"Pray to me,
and I will
answer you.
I will tell you
important
secrets you
have never
heard before."

Jeremiah 33:3 NCV

# INTRODUCTION

Whether you have made prayer a habit for many years or this is your first prayer devotional, inspiration is waiting for you in the daily prayers written here. Ultimately, prayer is a conversation with God. You don't need to use big words or recite long passages of Scripture. Just talk to God. Open your heart. He is listening to every word you say.

Some days your prayers may be filled with gratitude, some days with repentance, and some with need. Just lay your heart and your prayers at the Father's feet and wait for his powerful response.

May God bless you as you connect daily with him through prayer.

As you develop a habit of prayer, think about this:

**Praise.**

Begin by telling God how wonderful he is. Focus on which of his many attributes you are grateful for.

**Repentance.**

Before you present your needs to God, pause. Take a moment to examine your heart. If God reveals any unconfessed sin, bring it before him and ask for forgiveness.

**Ask.**

What do you need from your Father in heaven today? Ask him boldly; he is waiting to grant you the desires of your heart.

**Yield.**

Ask as if it will be done and yield to his will. Acknowledge he may know something you don't or have something even better in mind for you. Trust and accept whatever answer you receive.

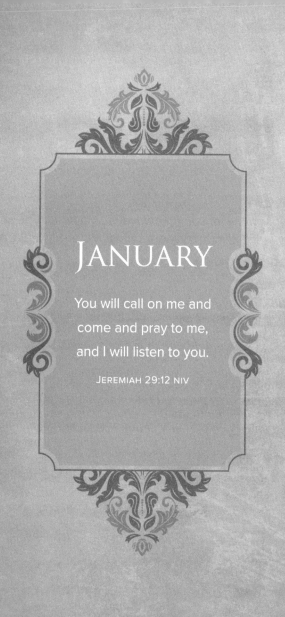

# JANUARY

You will call on me and
come and pray to me,
and I will listen to you.

JEREMIAH 29:12 NIV

# PERFECT PLAN

Many are the plans in a person's heart,
but it is the LORD's purpose that prevails.
PROVERBS 19:21 NIV

Almighty Father, King of the heavens and the earth, I
magnify your name and exalt you for your wisdom and
faithfulness. You have established your creation and set
forth your plans of restoration. You are most powerful, and
no one can thwart what you have decreed, despite their
best efforts. Your will absolutely will be done, your people
will be established as the head of all nations, and all
people will be blessed through Abraham's seed. You will
raise up a righteous remnant of people from all nations—
people who have sworn their allegiance to your kingdom
and sovereignty.

Lord, may I be found as one of these. I place my hope in
you, give my dreams and plans to you, and trust that you will
mold me into the man that you have desired since the dawn
of creation. I look forward to the crown of righteousness
you have prepared for those who diligently follow your
leadership and await the day of your promised restoration.
Be glorified in all the earth, oh Lord my God. Hallelujah
and amen!

**What purpose lies at the heart of God's will and
actions in your life?**

# CHOOSING WELL

Trust in the LORD with all your heart,
And lean not on your own understanding;
In all your ways acknowledge Him,
And He shall direct your paths.

PROVERBS 3:5-6 NKJV

Oh Father, I praise and glorify you as God and King. Your wisdom is wonderful beyond what I could imagine, and the way you have orchestrated redemption and restoration for the people of the world is magnificent. The more your Spirit highlights the intricacy and beauty of your plan, the more appreciation I gain for how inadequate my plans are. I trust in you, for your love is good, your plan is wise, and your rulership unquestioned.

Direct me down the path of righteousness, my God, and mold my heart. Increase my faith, Father, and cause me to more deeply await the fulfillment of the promises you have made. You know my desire to be active. Please give me the patience to wait on you and do as you desire, not as I would; to go where you point me, not in the direction I would choose. I entrust myself to you. May my offering be pleasing to you.

**Which direction is God's path headed? What is he leading you toward?**

# WORK THAT MATTERS

Whatever you do, work heartily,
as for the Lord and not for men.
COLOSSIANS 3:23 ESV

King of the heavens and the earth, I give you my heart, my soul, my mind, and my strength. In all my ways I want to see you satisfied with my work. I want you to see me as a man faithful in my commitment to your rulership. May my work be satisfying to you as you lead me by your Holy Spirit down the path of righteousness in this life, doing as you have ordered and trusting in your goodness. May I be a trustworthy caretaker of the tasks you set before me daily and may that help to serve as a reliable witness to others of my hope in your sovereign plans of restoration.

Lord, I pray as Jesus did that your kingdom would come soon, and that your will be done fully on the earth as it is done in the heavens. I pray that my desires would align with yours, and that you will be glorified in my life.

**Why is it important to work at all things as if for the Lord?**

# POSITIVE INFLUENCE

"Let your light shine before men in such a way
that they may see your good works,
and glorify your Father who is in heaven."

MATTHEW 5:16 NASB

God, you have set me to be a bearer of your image in the earth. Fill me with your Spirit so I may shine the truth of your character to all I encounter. May they see your goodness and be drawn to it. May people turn from the ways of the world and devote themselves to you. May they know the good news of your coming kingdom because of the example they see in me. You have molded me into your image.

Fill me with your love and compassion, with your faithfulness and devotion. May my calls to righteousness be tempered with care and empathy. May your light reflect off me like a mirror to all you would like to call to your kingdom.

**How is God glorified in the eyes of others by your good works?**

# SEND FRIENDS

If either of them falls down,
one can help the other up.
But pity anyone who falls
and has no one to help them up.

ECCLESIASTES 4:10 NIV

Father, nothing is better than walking together with friends of like mind and pursuits. You know how wonderful it is to walk in fellowship with others; you created humans to be able to do it. You desire companionship and the ability to share life with others. I ask for this in my own life. May I always have strong friends who walk with me, sharing in my joys and struggles.

Sometimes it can be too easy for a man to go his own way thinking he doesn't need anyone else, but you know this is false. Fill this need in my life, oh Lord. Set together friends who may be encouraged by each other and joyfully press each other toward the day of your coming. Thank you that you provide all my needs including this one.

**Consider how this passage relates to the idea that God "made them one" because he desired godly offspring.**

# BROUGHT LOW

When holy lovers of God cry out
to him with all their hearts,
the Lord will hear them and come to rescue them
from all their troubles.

PSALM 34:17 TPT

Lord, you have called all people to devote themselves to you. In the beginning, humanity turned from you to seek after their own desires and sensibilities. You have put forth the message to all nations that they should turn from this path and return to the one true God. You are drawing out a remnant of people from all nations who will have sworn their allegiance to you and who cry out to you for restoration and renewal.

Hear our cries, oh Lord. Restore your creation, fulfill your promises, and renew your people in your holy faithfulness. I long for your presence and need your sanctuary. Rescue me from the trials of this life and bring me through them in righteousness. Glorify your name in me.

**What might a delay in God's deliverance signify?**

# ABIDE

"Abide in me, and I in you.
As the branch cannot bear fruit by itself,
unless it abides in the vine,
neither can you, unless you abide in me."

JOHN 15:4 ESV

Father, I love that your Word reminds me of your good gifts and great promises. You are the worker of miracles. I receive my provision from you and every need is provided. Keep me near to you and give me the strength I need to continue to place my trust in you. You sustain those who hope in you, and you keep them through trials and through difficulty.

I give you my allegiance and place my hope in the certainty of your faithful promises. Produce in me the fruit of your Spirit and grant me the privilege of yielding other faithful adherents to the great promise of your coming kingdom. I am pleased to serve you, my God, and to act in anticipation of your coming.

**What fruit do you see as a result of abiding in him?**

# FULLY COMMITTED

"Devote yourselves completely to the LORD our God, walking in his statutes and keeping his commandments, as at this day."
1 KINGS 8:61 NRSV

I am so thankful to you, Father, for the goodness you have shown me, for the offer of peace you have extended, for the mercy you have poured out, and for the forgiveness that paves my path. I give myself to you with all my hopes and desires.

I love to show you honor through the commands you have set down; may your Holy Spirit strengthen me to maintain my allegiance and to endure fully along this path of life. I choose devotion to you over the things of this world. Deliver me safely to the day when you establish your righteous rule in the earth so I may enjoy the fruit of your power. Hallelujah and amen.

**What does it mean to be devoted completely to the Lord?**

# Deliver Me

"Lead us not into temptation,
but deliver us from the evil one."
Matthew 6:13 NIV

Lord, fill me with your Holy Spirit and provide the means of
escape from temptations whenever the enemy presents
them. Magnify the hope of your coming kingdom in my eyes
so I remain steadfast in my pursuit of your promises. Then, I
will not turn after the fleeting distractions with which the evil
one attempts to entice me.

Skillfully guide me along the path of life and sustain me with
the nourishment of your instruction. I will glorify you in the
day of your visitation and exalt your name to the nations.
May your great mercies be renewed every day and your
leadership prove faithful each morning.

**What makes the evil one's temptations so
frequently effective?**

# ACCOUNTABLE

Each one must answer for himself
and give a personal account of his own life before God.
ROMANS 14:12 TPT

My Lord, I am humbled that you have established humans to govern the earth as your image bearers. You have given us the responsibility to rule righteously in accordance with your wisdom. You have not left us without instruction, giving us your Scriptures and pouring your Holy Spirit on all who ask for it. You have desired godly governance to bless the people of the earth and wisely utilize its resources.

Give me the gift of your wisdom to know how to act appropriately in the jurisdiction you have given me, no matter how small that area is. Grant me the ability to make wise decisions and to take this responsibility seriously, loving and caring for others as I direct them to the wisdom and mercy of your good news. Fill me to overflowing with the goodness of your hopes and desires, so I will reflect them in the choices I make. Thank you for the great honor of entrusting me with this task.

**Why are we held responsible for the things we have done in this life?**

# So Much Grace

From his fullness we have all received,
grace upon grace.
JOHN 1:16 NRSV

Father, you have been so kind to your people, though all the nations have been so faithless to you. You have set down your instruction; you pour out your Spirit, letting us know your desires and plans. Even the stars declare the majesty of your good news and grand promises. I give you glory for the magnitude of your power and goodness, for how pervasive they are, and for the depths of your wisdom in the way you have set creation to work.

Teach me the depths of your ways so I may better understand the gift you have promised and maintain this path of righteousness more diligently. Above all else, thank you for the mercy you have extended to me to allow me to approach you despite my great unworthiness. I come from people who have rejected you and turned to gods who have not served you. Continue to grant me mercy until the day of your return, for I long to glorify you amid the joyous assembly.

**What is the purpose behind God's multitude of good gifts?**

# LONELINESS

Even if my father and mother abandon me,
the LORD will hold me close.
PSALM 27:10 NLT

Father you are good to me and have granted me the right
to be called according to your name. Give me the strength
to maintain my allegiance to you and the promise of your
coming kingdom. Remain with me even if my friends and
family abandon me for your sake and vindicate your name
in their eyes because of your faithfulness. May your ways be
magnified before the nations as you fulfill your promises to
establish your people.

May your blessing flow to all nations as the mighty rivers
flow to the seas. Your promises are yes and amen because
of the nature of your love and faithfulness to your creation.
You will establish those you call yours. I long to be counted
among them when you come. Be exalted and magnified in
the earth, so that both heaven and earth sing your praises in
a unified voice.

**Who does the Lord call his friends?**

# REFRESH AND RESTORE

It is in vain that you rise up early
and go late to rest,
eating the bread of anxious toil;
for he gives to his beloved sleep.
PSALM 127:2 ESV

My Lord and King, I put my trust in you to care for my daily needs. You have the power and the faithfulness to look after your own, and you even pour out your blessing on your enemies, so I have no need to fear for my life. Your promises of provision to those who remain faithful to your good news are beyond compare.

Teach me your way and show me the path you have set before me, guiding me to the work you desire me to complete in this life instead of constantly striving merely to preserve this fleeting life. You have set us to work with our hands to bring forth our food, yet that should not be my all-consuming focus. Mold and shape me into the man you want me to be so I glorify you and thank you in all your ways.

**Upon what is your hope ultimately fixed?**

# A Heart that Would

I plead with you to give your bodies to God because of all he has done for you. Let them be a living and holy sacrifice—the kind he will find acceptable. This is truly the way to worship him.

ROMANS 12:1 NLT

I give myself to you and devote myself to your commands and edicts, oh great King. Be pleased with the offering I give you, though I am not much in myself. You have given and you may take away, and I am at your mercy and your service. Accomplish your good works in me and through me to all the people you have set in my path.

Give me the wisdom and ability to be faithful to your commands and help me to continue working to see others devote themselves to your promises. May the resources you entrust to my care produce an ample return; show me the way to utilize them in your service. I am eager to set my attention on the tasks you see fit to give me and to complete them to your glorification.

**What kind of work does God find pleasing?**

# ACCEPTING OTHERS

As it is in your heart, let it be in mine. Christ accepted you, so you
should accept each other, which will bring glory to God.
ROMANS 15:7 NCV

God fill me with the desire to befriend and be kind to my
fellow believer. Help me to defer to their needs and not
assert my own rights when these things conflict. Remind
me of the love and care you have given me and how you
have not asserted your right to treat me the way my actions
deserve. If anyone is worthy of getting their way, it is you,
Father, yet you refrain from making it happen so your wrath
does not consume us all.

You have desired godly offspring to fill the earth with
righteous people, so you have set out to draw those who
mistreat you to turn from their ways and be saved. Set my
desires to treat others similarly so you may have the time to
mold them—and me—into the people you will be pleased
with. Thank you for your goodness and for giving me favor
that I don't deserve.

**Why is it important to restrain the desire to assert our
rights in this world?**

# RUN TO WIN

Do you not know that in a race all the runners run, but only one gets the prize? Run in such a way as to get the prize.
1 CORINTHIANS 9:24 NIV

Train me and strengthen me, my Lord, so I may be diligent and live my life fully devoted to attaining life in the next age. Don't let me get complacent with small victories in this life as if they were the objective at which I was aiming. I am not aiming to see miracles happen, though they empower me. I am not aiming to be a prophet, though prophecy propels me. I am not aiming to be a preacher, though teaching equips me.

Give me righteous instruction and sound discipline that prepares me to endure the pain and weariness I will inevitably face. I won't be satisfied with the temporary rewards of this life but will press forward to receive the full promises you have set before those who will endure in cultivating righteousness until the end of the age.

**Have you ever thought that receiving the prize of life was a foregone conclusion? What is the reason for the Scriptures continuous reminder to keep running?**

# FORGIVEN

"Whenever you stand praying, forgive, if you have anything against anyone; so that your Father in heaven may also forgive you your trespasses."

MARK 11:25 NRSV

Forgive me of my affronts to your rulership and sovereignty, mighty King. I bow before you in humility with the knowledge of the ways I have worked against your will. I have not kept your authority in the forefront of my mind but have instead taken my own path to fulfill my own desires. To you and you alone am I indebted, for you are the ruler over all things.

Lord, grant that I will also forgive my neighbors for things I perceive have been done against me. Help me to treat them with the honor and respect I am seeking from you. Fill my heart with your forgiving attitude and conform my spirit to your compassionate ways. Be glorified in the earth, oh Lord, because of your great love.

**What is it about forgiving others that opens the door for God to forgive us?**

# GIFTS IN DISGUISE

Give thanks in all circumstances; for this is the will of God
in Christ Jesus for you.
1 THESSALONIANS 5:18 ESV

Father, I am thankful to you for your great mercy and love
that you have poured out through the good news of Jesus'
death, resurrection, and return. How good you have been
to me is difficult even for me to pinpoint, and my heart
gives you praise and thanks for your goodness. Help me
to also thank you in those times when I do not see any
good, helping me to recognize that you are using the
circumstances of life to mold and shape me into the kind of
human you have always meant me to be.

You have said that you work all things together to benefit
those whom you have called according to your purpose.
Thank you that you remain by my side, working all things
to such an end, so that in the day of your coming, I will be
rewarded by you with everlasting life.

**What are some things you are experiencing right
now that don't seem good or helpful? Can you see
how they might be used to form a righteous heart
within you?**

# INSPIRE ME

God created great sea creatures and every living thing that
scurries and swarms in the water, and every sort of bird—
each producing offspring of the same kind.
And God saw that it was good.
GENESIS 1:21 NLT

Your works are magnificent and deserving of praise. Your power and creativity are amazing. You are without equal, oh Lord, and your majesty is exceedingly wonderful. I am moved by your works and the way you have set creation in motion; you sustain it by your will and your desire is to see it prosper. You have established your plans with amazing wisdom and the path you have set for salvation is inspiring in how it builds righteous character.

I thank you for your Holy Spirit that encourages and strengthens me. It also reminds me of the wonder of your works and the multitude of ways you have been faithful to your Word and your people. Keep me focused on your good works and the majesty of your coming kingdom so I won't become anxious about the troubles of the world. I rejoice to see you at work, oh Lord. Be glorified!

**How has God's creativity inspired your own imagination?**

# No Compromise

"If you love me, obey my commandments."
JOHN 14:15 NLT

Oh Lord my God, how majestic is your name in all the earth! Your commandments inspire wonder and amazement in me. You have established goodness and righteousness by your great wisdom. I ask for your Spirit to fill me with the desire to obey you, to show forth my devotion to you and your rulership by my willing obedience to your ways.

Help me to stand strong in the dictates of your righteousness, Father, for they are not burdensome or tiring, but they will lead me along the path to the refreshing time of your promised restoration. I hope to follow you with all my desire and strength, so help me to love you with everything I have.

**What are the commandments Jesus refers to here?**

# RENEWED STRENGTH

Those who wait for the LORD shall renew their strength,
they shall mount up with wings like eagles,
they shall run and not be weary,
they shall walk and not faint.

ISAIAH 40:31 NRSV

Oh Lord, I long for you and ache for the revelation of your great work in the earth. I cry out to you to fulfill your promises. How long must we wait, oh God? Yet I will wait for you and look for you; I will anticipate your arrival. Like a child awaiting the arrival of their father from a long trip, I am eager with anticipation. The day of your coming will be filled with rejoicing and glory.

Give me the grace and patience to remain faithful until your arrival. Help me to be steadfast and not fall asleep as I so often can. May your Spirit be a favorable gift to me that strengthens me while I wait. I long to be satisfied with you and your great promises.

**What is the purpose of waiting on the Lord?**

# SEASON OF GRIEF

Since we believe that Jesus died and rose again,
even so, through Jesus, God will bring with him
those who have fallen asleep.

1 THESSALONIANS 4:14 ESV

Loving Father, you know my heart right now, how it aches
for my lost loved one. The hole that their absence creates
is significant, and I don't always know how to deal with
it. I long for their presence once again. Father, I don't
understand why we are made to create such bonds with
other people to then have those relationships torn apart
through death. It is a great pain to endure!

Father, I pray your Spirit would remind me of the good
news of your restoration and resurrection. It is so easy
to fall into the trap of believing that this separation is
permanent even when my mind tells me I will be reunited
one day. Help me to see this separation as a temporary
departure so I may be comforted by your good news.
Magnify the truth of your restorative promises within
me so I will not wither away under this cloud of grief.
Thank you for understanding what we face in this life and
providing a means of comfort and reunion.

**In what way can seeing the loss of a loved one as
akin to a lengthy road trip rather than a permanent
departure change the way we deal with that separation?**

# LOVING WELL

"A new commandment I give to you, that you love one another, even as I have loved you, that you also love one another."
JOHN 13:34 NASB

Father God, when I consider the ways you show your love to me, in the various ways you provide for my basic needs, in the fact that you have remembered me even though my ancestors forgot you, in the extravagance of how you have provided for me to be restored, and in the way you give of yourself—I stand in awe! How can I love others in such a fashion? How do I follow your example?

Strengthen my Spirit to reach out with what I have to offer. Help me to care for my neighbor even when it is not necessary for my own benefit. Open my eyes to truly see others rather than allowing my self-interest to narrow my perspective. May others see your love in the way I love.

**How is this command Jesus gives a new command?**

# CASTING BURDENS

Cast your burden on the LORD,
And He shall sustain you;
He shall never permit the righteous to be moved.
PSALM 55:22 NKJV

Dear Lord, take from me the burdens I so easily carry. Remind me of your goodness and the temporary nature of this life and the cares of this world, considering the greatness of your promises for the age to come. You are more than able to care for me in times of need now, but even if you don't always come through in the ways I think I need, you have promised to sustain me and to help me find my way. Help me to rest in that knowledge and not be moved to worry about the difficult things I face and endure now.

I pray you will be lifted in my thoughts as the great King you are, so I can rest assured of the goodness of your promises which are certain and true because of your power and authority to bring them to pass. Magnificent Lord, I am so grateful for your ways and your support.

**What burdens do you carry that seem so big now but actually pale in light of God's promised hope?**

# MERCY UPON MERCY

"They are blessed who show mercy to others,
for God will show mercy to them."
MATTHEW 5:7 NCV

Merciful Father, strengthen me to be merciful with my words, with my attitudes, and with the way I treat others. Remind me of your mercy so I will live mercifully with others. You are the greatest of all, and from you all good things have come; yet, you have been affronted more than any other. You have received more animosity and rebellion than any, but you treat your creation with mercy, restraining your justice and calling people to a saving repentance.

I want to be like you, Father, doing good to all, including those who mistreat me or who are careless in their ways. May my merciful demeanor help attract others to your graciousness for their benefit and salvation.

**How does your merciful attitude affect God's attitude toward you?**

# Quick to Listen

Take note of this: Everyone should be quick to listen, slow to speak and slow to become angry.

JAMES 1:19 NIV

Father, you are grand in all your ways and in your majesty. What am I before you? I hope to learn from the wisdom of your Holy Spirit. Help me to wait patiently before you and listen to what you have to say. Help me to listen to people's experiences and process things that I have not personally seen. Let my words be few before you and others, not eager to exalt my own experiences and thoughts as of first importance.

Prepare me, Lord, to receive instruction that is in accordance with your Word and the Spirit in which it was given. May I also be slow to grow angry with others, but instead treat them as better than myself, not willing to disparage others easily without knowing more about their own plight. Fill me with your graciousness and patience as a sign of my belief in your promised judgment and restoration.

**What could be the consequence of being slow to listen, quick to speak, and quick to become angry?**

# FOREVER GIFTS

When God chooses someone and graciously imparts gifts to him,
they are never rescinded.

ROMANS 11:29 TPT

God, you are a good father and creator showing kindness to me in so many ways, small and large. You have made me in your image and have given me gifts that are uniquely mine. Thank you for your favorable disposition toward me. Help me to make use of these gifts and not to squander or take them for granted. Fill me with desire and ideas of how to utilize the gifts you have given me. You had a purpose for me receiving them; I ask for your help in using them.

I am amazed at how fearfully and wonderfully you have made me, and I want to make good use of the resources you have put at my disposal especially to glorify you with them. Glorious Father, make your will and plans clear to me so I will not use these gifts in a meaningless fashion. Exalt your name in the earth and help me to declare your good news with the tools you have provided me.

**How does the steadfastness of God's gifts encourage you as you walk in faithfulness today?**

# While I Wait

Be strong, and let your heart take courage,
all you who wait for the LORD!
PSALM 31:24 ESV

My Lord and my God, as I look around me and see what the world holds, I am encouraged by the beauty of your creation, yet I long to see the renewal of your promised restoration. I wait expectantly for your coming! Grant me peace of mind and heart when the walls of the world seem to squeeze around me. I know that the world cannot prevent what you are going to reveal in the day of your coming, so I take courage.

Help me to enjoy the beauty that surrounds me, Father, and not be overcome with despair at that which is ugly or dark. I love your good works and the miracles you have established, both those that occur daily and those that you have promised to bring.

**What exactly is it that encourages you while you wait for God?**

# EVERY GOOD THING

Every good thing given and every perfect gift is from above, coming down from the Father of lights, with whom there is no variation or shifting shadow.

JAMES 1:17 NASB

Father of lights, you are magnificent in all your ways and in the faithfulness with which you guide me along the paths of righteousness. You know what I need; you are full of wisdom, my Creator. You give me what is good for life and for righteousness while leading me away from what is bad for me.

When I look at the creation you have made, and the environment in which you have placed me—how you made it to reproduce food and life-giving materials, how you set forth the means to have fellowship and to be encouraged—I am grateful for the depths of your imagination and the ways in which you give gifts to me and all who live within your domain.

**Why is a gift characterized as good when it comes from the Father when it may be bad when it comes from another source?**

# Speak of Love

If you confess with your mouth the Lord Jesus and believe in your heart that God has raised Him from the dead, you will be saved. For with the heart one believes unto righteousness, and with the mouth confession is made unto salvation.

ROMANS 10: 9–10 NKJV

Loving God, your faithfulness has not failed, and your promises remain "yes and amen." You have established Jesus to be the ruler of all the earth, yet he was killed according to your purposes. Even so, you resurrected him from the dead and displayed to all the earth, to all humanity, and to the depths of my heart that your love speaks forth from the depths of death, and you will establish your good plans according to your great power.

Your love and great kindness to humanity are left obvious to all who are made aware, and I will declare the truth of Jesus' restoration, eagerly awaiting the day of his return.

**How does Jesus' resurrection testify that God is love to your heart?**

# GENTLENESS

Remind the people to be subject to rulers and authorities, to be
obedient, to be ready to do whatever is good, to slander no one,
to be peaceable and considerate, and always to be
gentle toward everyone.

TITUS 3:1–2 NIV

Glorious Father, you are gracious and marvelous in your
ways. I trust you with my life and wait for the reward you
have promised in the day of your coming. Grant me the
peace of mind and spirit that results in kindness and
goodness to all I encounter. You have established your will
and authority, and I put my trust in your choices. May the
leaders you have put in place rule righteously before you
and give me the grace to be obedient to them as I would
be to you.

I know that you are the great King and judge who will punish
all wicked activity and put an end to the wicked ways of men
in the earth, so I will be satisfied in the day of your glory.
I wait on you for you are the righteous judge and you will
make right judgments. Your heart desires to show mercy,
yet you will not endure evil forever. I can rest soundly in this
knowledge and even offer peace to my enemies because I
know their actions will not be ignored.

**Why are you encouraged to be obedient, kind, and
peaceable in all circumstances?**

# February

Look to the LORD
and his strength;
seek his face always.

1 CHRONICLES 16:11 NIV

# First Stone

When they persisted in asking Him, He straightened up, and said to them, "He who is without sin among you, let him be the first to throw a stone at her."

JOHN 8:7 NASB

Lord God, you have forgiven and been merciful to me in so many ways. I want to be kind and caring for others in a similar way. You don't desire to see anyone destroyed; you'd rather see them stop doing the things they do against you, turn to follow you, and be redeemed. Give me the ability to see others as being just as deserving of mercy as I have been, and, in considering your true mercy, to be willing to stand with them in the truth so they may follow the path of righteousness.

Help me follow Jesus' example and stand up for the wicked, calling them to turn away from their ways while being willing to accept even death for their sake. I know that you have shown me great mercy, and I will not act arrogantly against others. May your name be glorified in the earth because of your great mercy.

**How do you balance a merciful attitude with a call to repentance?**

# ALL I NEED

My God will supply every need of yours according to
his riches in glory in Christ Jesus.
PHILIPPIANS 4:19 ESV

Loving Father, I put my trust in you to provide for me.
Though it is easy to put my hope in my own strength or
ability, in the jobs I can do, the work I can perform, or the
occupations I can make pay, I choose to rely on you for my
needs because you are steadfast and sure in your provision.
Whatever I may set my hand to do may fail, but you will
succeed, so I trust in you instead of myself.

Lord, you know how my heart wavers. Show me
your lovingkindness and remind me of your works of
righteousness and faithfulness both in history and in my own
life. I easily forget your goodness in the flow of life, so I ask
you to keep showing me your provision day by day so I do
not forget. I long for your coming, and I know that in that day
all my needs will be met more substantially than I can hope
or imagine. Thank you for the encouragement of your
good news!

**In light of the good news, what does it mean for God to
supply your needs?**

# SIMPLE PLEASURES

I've learned from my experience
that God protects the childlike and humble ones.
For I was broken and brought low,
but he answered me and came to my rescue!

PSALM 116:6 TPT

Father, thank you for your help when life comes crashing around me. When these things happen to me, I am reminded that I am not so great and awesome but am only a mere mortal walking through this world. I am humbled and put in a place that causes me to cry out to you in need. I am so grateful to you who hears that cry and responds.

You do not answer those who are puffed up in pride at their circumstances rather than being humble. You sustain the broken and those who recognize that they have no standing to demand a benefit from the world. You will come to them and rescue them from this life of struggle and establish them in the restoration of all creation. Therefore, I will glorify you as one who owes everything to you, for you have given freely to me out of your incomparable favor.

**In the context of humility, brokenness, and low-standing, what does it mean to be childlike?**

# POWER SUPPLY

He gives power to the faint,
and strengthens the powerless.
ISAIAH 40:29 NRSV

Father, you are beautiful and wonderful in your ways.
You refresh me with your Spirit and lift me up with your
goodness. Strengthen my weakness, Lord, and make me
able to stand with you. Help me to walk even when I feel
like hiding away. I do not feel able to continue, but you are
more than capable to sustain me. Let me drink deeply of the
living water you promise to give to those who put their trust
in you. I need the bread you offer so I will be wholly revived.

Be glorified, my God, in the testimony of the weak who have
cried out to you, for our stories will tell of the faithfulness
and surety of your greatness.

**What is the goal of the strengthening that God gives
when you call on him in weakness?**

# No Small Miracle

You are the God who performs miracles;
you display your power among the peoples.
PSALM 77:14 NIV

Oh Lord, when I consider the works of your hands—the extent of your creation, the way you rescued your chosen ones from bondage and delivered them into the land of their promise—I am awestruck by your miraculous works! You have made yourself known to the world, and you declare your majesty. You have promised a total restoration of the earth, and you confirm the testimony of this promise through signs and wonders performed among the nations of the earth.

Lord, I pray that you would be magnified in my life now in just such a way. Your works are great; I pray for your miraculous touch in these circumstances now. Magnify your name and promises by your great works.

**How can you remind yourself of God's miraculous works each day?**

# INSPIRED TO PLEASE

"Be careful! When you do good things, don't do them in front of people to be seen by them. If you do that, you will have no reward from your Father in heaven."

MATTHEW 6:1 NCV

My Father, you are great in all your ways and glorious to behold. May my desire be to please you with my actions. I am so easily swayed to try to gain approval from other people, but it is your approval that is more valuable than any riches or personal accolades I might gain from being thought of well by people. You are the one who rewards those who do well in your sight with everlasting life. Help me to remember that people are just like me and not the standard of approval.

When I am consumed with being acceptable to other people, I often lose sight of your great promises and the wisdom of a life lived in anticipation of your coming. Father, I pray you will be pleased with my offering and glorified in my testimony. Let my works be seen in your throne room and my praise come from your mouth.

**What do you think is wrong with seeking the approval of men?**

# CONFIDENCE

Do not throw away your confidence, which has a great reward.
HEBREWS 10:35 NCV

Oh Lord and great God, you are holy and worthy to be praised in every way. I exalt your great name, and long to see your face with my own eyes in the land of the living. You deserve all honor and praise, exalted Father, for your works of righteousness are magnificent. You have established your plans with certainty and will surely bring them to fruition.

You will fulfill what you have promised with great power. My heart desires to be with you in that day and to partake in your great reward. Draw me close by your Holy Spirit and mold me into the character of your Son, Jesus. May my life model his and my desires mimic his which are also yours. Be glorified in the earth, oh God, just as you are in the heavens.

**How can you throw away your confidence?**

# REMAIN FAITHFUL

If we are faithless, he remains faithful—for he cannot deny himself.
2 TIMOTHY 2:13 ESV

Glorious Father, I give you my thanks for being so faithful. You are true to your Word and promises; you do not deviate from them. Help me to be like you in faithfulness. I ask for your Holy Spirit to fill me with wisdom and understanding to be faithful in all my dealings. You do not reward a person who is two-faced and cannot be trusted.

You have called me to be a person whose word is yes or no and can be trusted to follow through. This is your character and you desire to see that in me as well. Forgive me, Lord, for the times when I have broken faith with you and with others. Restore me to faithfulness for your name's sake, so a true testimony of your character may go out to the world.

**To what promises will God be faithful because he cannot deny himself? Are they only good promises, or are some less desirable? How does that affect your way of living before him?**

# EVERYTHING CHANGES

Be diligent in these matters; give yourself wholly to them,
so that everyone may see your progress.
1 TIMOTHY 4:15 NIV

Lord, you have given me your Word and your Spirit so
I might grow in maturity and character in the mold of
Jesus. Thank you for your benevolent provision. May they
continually bear fruit in my life so I may be found like Jesus
in your sight—righteous, humble, and self-sacrificial. May
others see the way I am changing so they may glorify you
now and in the day of your visitation. I want them to also be
saved from the coming day of wrath. Lift me up so I will not
stumble on the rugged trails; help make my paths straight as
they lead me to you.

You are so very gracious to me and I lift my eyes to you,
devoting myself to your ways and teachings so I finish this
race you have set before me. When I started it, I was in no
condition to finish it, but you have supplied me with all that I
need to grow in godliness and faith. Thank you, my Father!

**How has the Lord been bringing about change within
you, and for what purpose is he doing that work?**

# LIGHT, LOVE, AND TRUTH

Peter and the apostles replied,
"We must obey God rather than any human."
ACTS 5:29 NLT

Father, many things of this life seek to make me turn from following your way, but I ask for the light of your truth to shine on my path. Guide me in the way of peace and righteousness and strengthen me to do as you have commanded. It is so easy to turn aside and do as others do, to follow in their steps and try to keep peace with them instead of doing what you have called me to do. Help me to follow you in these instances while showing true love to those around me.

Help me to testify to others that the reason for my going a different way is because of your great promises; that you are returning to restore the earth and you will bring justice with you. May your Spirit highlight the truth of your everlasting love to all who encounter me because of the testimony of my life and word.

**What message do you send to others when you choose to obey what you have received from God rather than obey the commands the world gives?**

# THE MIRROR

If anyone is in Christ, there is a new creation: everything old has passed away; see, everything has become new!
2 CORINTHIANS 5:17 NRSV

Renew my spirit according to your great and marvelous works, my God. Cause my desires to be turned back to the path of righteousness as you intended them to do in the beginning. Make my paths straight as they become aimed directly at the renewal you have promised. May I live now according to the nature of the hope you have declared is certain to come.

In the power of your Holy Spirit and according to his direction, I will reflect the glory of Jesus' character and ways. He is the second Adam, the one who exemplified precisely what you had always desired humanity to be in the earth, and I put my trust in you that you will resurrect all who seek to attain to his example. May my desire to pursue false and futile goals fade into the distance as I set my eyes fully on the reward of the resurrected Messiah.

**What aspects of your life and pursuits still need to be conformed to the image of Jesus?**

# NOT GOOD

I know what it is to be in need, and I know what it is to have
plenty. I have learned the secret of being content in any
and every situation, whether well fed or hungry,
whether living in plenty or in want.

PHILIPPIANS 4:12 NIV

You have shown me the key to true joy, oh Lord—the
knowledge of your faithful love that fulfills your promises.
I can endure anything in this life, good or bad, because
you are teaching me that attaining a place in the coming
resurrection is the true goal that produces happiness.
Though many things in this life attempt to tear me down,
to beat me, to destroy me, I still live in joy and strength
because the promise of your resurrection and restoration is
certain to be fulfilled.

You will do what you have promised, and that knowledge
fills me with true hope. May my life reflect that knowledge
and may other people see it in me and believe my words.

**What encourages you when your circumstances start
to drain your contentment and joy?**

# LET YOU IN

Search me, O God, and know my heart;
test me and know my anxious thoughts.
PSALM 139:23 NLT

Father, I ask you to transform the motivations of my heart and aim me at the true goal of this life. You have not brought me into this life for this life alone, but ever since the beginning, you have placed the restoration as the true goal. The righteous ones who have come before all looked for the fulfillment of your promises in the day of resurrection, and I want to be counted among them.

Search me out, oh God, and deal with the impurity in my pursuits and the desire to preserve everything I possibly can in this life. You value life, and I adore the way you have sought to enrich our experience, but you also know that this life is merely a vapor compared to the glory you have in store. You desire me to testify of your coming grandeur through the way I give my life for others, especially my enemies. I will serve you diligently in this. Be magnified in me.

**What is the reason for asking God to search the depths of your being?**

# YOU ARE LOVE

He who does not love does not know God, for God is love.
1 JOHN 4:8 NKJV

Teach me the depths of your love, Father, so I may love others in truth. We so flippantly use the word and so few of us really know what it means to love others. You are faithful to your promises and do not turn back on your obligations. You call those who have turned against you to turn back, and you warn people in advance of the end result of the path they have chosen to take. You are careful to watch after those who have been entrusted to your care and you do not leave them or forsake them.

How can I be called according to your name and purposes if I am not trustworthy? Help me to care for your people as you do; I desire to follow in your steps. May your name be exalted in the eyes of the nations because of the love your people show in accordance with your example.

**What are some differences between the way God loves and the way the world loves?**

# ONE HEART

"I will give them one heart, and put a new spirit within them.
And I will take the heart of stone out of their flesh
and give them a heart of flesh."

EZEKIEL 11:19 NASB

Fill me with your desires and will so I may follow your way, Lord my God. May I not be hardened against your Spirit, but may he draw me close to you. Mold me into the character of Jesus, the model in whose image humans were created and whose life serves as our example. Help me not to be double minded in my way, looking both at the hope of your good news and also at the fleeting satisfaction of this life. Make my purpose conform with your purposes and my desires conform to your will.

I am amazed that you have made so many different people, yet our goals could be aligned together, aimed at the one purpose of reconciliation and restoration you have set in your good will. Cause me to be unified with you and with your people that we glorify you in peace and harmony in the day of your visitation.

**What is the one aim that God wants to instill in you?**

# EVERY OPPORTUNITY

Don't allow yourselves to be weary or disheartened in planting
good seeds, for the season of reaping the wonderful harvest
you've planted is coming!
GALATIANS 6:9 TPT

Father, do you understand the futility we feel at not seeing
the fulfillment of the promise you have given? I am weak and
need your strengthening. Show me a sign that the race I am
running is not a vain one. Fill me with the courage to push
through discouragement so I may see the Son rise. Renew
within me the joy of your salvation and cause my eyes to
become focused on the day I will attain it.

You have set a day when you will judge the acts of all
people and reward them according to their works. Then I
will see the fruit of my labor and enjoy with you the beautiful
produce of my work. Set my will like iron to pursue that day,
knowing that the things I see you do today are merely signs
of what will be. Thank you for not leaving me to walk out this
faith alone. You walk with me.

**What are some ways that weariness manifests
in your life?**

# ILLUSION OF CONTROL

Give yourselves completely to God. Stand against the devil,
and the devil will run from you.

JAMES 4:7 NASB

Great God and King of the heavens and earth, you have
established the right way and set forth your good path. You
alone have the sovereignty to make real what you desire to
bring forth. I have been deceived that my will is attainable,
and even when it seems I have gained what I desire, when
it is outside of your righteous will, it vanishes and leaves
me dissatisfied.

You are the one who truly deserves my allegiance even over
my own desires, hopes, and dreams. Transform these things
within me and set my hope on gaining your desires, hopes,
and dreams. Make me impervious to the attacks of the
enemy. I submit to your will and rulership; the accusations
of the enemy will not put me to shame.

**What is God's goal for you in this life?**

# Anger Rising

"In your anger do not sin": Do not let the sun go down
while you are still angry.
EPHESIANS 4:26 NIV

Father, help me to be righteously affected when sin creeps into my life and the lives of those with whom I commune. Give me the strength, by your Holy Spirit, to confront places in my life where unrighteousness sneaks in as well as the humility to respond tenderly to the Spirit's rebukes. May my life be continuously set apart to and for you, so you may be glorified in the day that you come. May I be ready to rejoice at your coming rather than being afraid as those who are unrepentant will be.

Fill me with your righteous indignation that may lead to repentance but without condemning others. Help me to draw out bitterness from my character and replace it with the sweet nectar of your Spirit. Thank you for calling me to repentance and providing a means by which I can be saved from your coming wrath.

**What do the Scriptures mean by not sinning
in your anger?**

# MEASURED STEPS

We also pray that you will be strengthened with all his glorious power so you will have all the endurance and patience you need.

COLOSSIANS 1:11 NLT

Dear Lord, I ask you to strengthen me in the grace of your Spirit with wisdom, patience, and understanding to guide my steps and straighten the path that leads to the day in which I have set all of my hope. Exert your power, oh Lord, in ways that remind me of your coming restoration, setting signposts before me that refresh my confidence in your promised salvation.

You have set your Spirit as a counselor and teacher and have provided power to overcome many obstacles in the world so your people might see them and be encouraged to press forward through difficulty to inherit your promises. Lord, continue to strengthen me and work in the lives of other believers so they are strengthened to press forward as well. I love to see your work in the world!

**In what way does God's glorious power strengthen endurance and patience your life?**

# PURSUED BY GOODNESS

Why would I fear the future?
For your goodness and love pursue me all the days of my life.
Then afterward, when my life is through,
I'll return to your glorious presence to be forever with you!
PSALM 23:6 TPT

Loving Father, I thank you that you are persistent in your patience with me. Do not let me fall away but give me strength to continue down the path of righteousness you have established, and I will not fear what the future holds. I will rejoice in the restoration you have promised for you have sustained me with your goodness and righteous love.

I depend on you, my Father, to keep me safe and to deliver me into your presence at the revelation of your kingdom. Treat me as a beloved son, oh Lord, so that I will not be led astray. I glorify you for your many mercies and faithful love, and in the day of your appearing, I will rejoice with the nations at the wedding feast of the Lamb.

**You might find yourself afraid of many things, but what fearful thing does the future actually hold?**

# SEPARATED FROM GUILT

Since we have been justified by faith, we have peace with God
through our Lord Jesus Christ.
ROMANS 5:1 ESV

Lord God, I am humbled and overwhelmed at your mercy and the way you have provided for me to be found not guilty of my transgressions against your rulership. Thank you for sending Jesus to become sin for me so I could be given the opportunity to turn away from sin and be freed from penalty. I see now that you are the God and King over all the earth and that I owe all allegiance to you, first and foremost. I trust in you and believe in your coming restoration of the rightful order of leadership on the earth.

Thank you for making peace with me even though I have so often warred against your commands. You have established a day in which you will judge the earth, and I declare my allegiance to the King of Israel, ruler over all nations. Magnificent Father, I pray your name will be exalted in all the earth just as in the heavens!

**Jesus asked, "When the Son of Man returns, will he find faith on the earth?" What do you think he means?**

# Far Away

In God, whose word I praise,
In God I have put my trust;
I shall not be afraid.
What can mere man do to me?

PSALM 56:4 NASB

I exalt your name, oh Lord my God, for you are wondrous
in all your ways. You have made an unbelievable plan for
saving the world and bringing restoration to the earth. You
have established your people according to your good will,
and you give the call to turn from evil to all people of all
nations so they may also be restored and renewed. Even
so, the rulers of the nations rage against you and they
war against your holy people. Strengthen your people—
strengthen me—against the wrath of men.

Lord, you know the fearsomeness of men's hatred from your
experience in the garden of Gethsemane, yet you endured
it for the sake of the promise of resurrection. Fill me with
courage to endure the attacks of your enemies. Help me to
overcome fear because I know the truth of your faithfulness
to fulfill your promises. In time, I know that you will reign in
righteousness over all the earth, and peace will flow your
holy mountain.

**How does trusting God quiet your fears?**

# RESTRAINT

"Put your sword back in its place," Jesus said to him,
"for all who draw the sword will die by the sword.
Do you think I cannot call on my Father, and he will at once
put at my disposal more than twelve legions of angels."
MATTHEW 26:52–53 NIV

Almighty God, ruler and sustainer of the whole earth, I am awestruck with the restraint you exhibit. The master of all creation looks about and sees unspeakable wickedness throughout the earth, people acting in defiance of you and what you know to be good for the world, yet you withhold your judgment. You have said that you do not delight in destroying the wicked, but in seeing them turn from evil and find salvation in your sight.

Develop this same heart of restraint and mercy within me so I mimic your compassion for others. Help me to testify to the wicked of the earth the goodness of your patience that gives extra time for people to turn and give their allegiance to you. May I be controlled in my wrath knowing that you are controlled in yours and that you have set a day for judgment. Thank you for your great wisdom.

**How does God's restraint in attacking those who hate him affect your daily faith walk?**

# MOVE ME

When He saw the multitudes, He was moved with compassion
for them, because they were weary and scattered,
like sheep having no shepherd.
MATTHEW 9:36 NKJV

Fill me with your heart of compassion and mercy, Father,
and help me to care for others as thoroughly as you do.
Help me not to get overwhelmed at the needs I see—for I
know that I am not the savior of the world—but give me eyes
to see what is within my control and be proactive enough
to address it. Moreover, help me to see people's deeper
needs: for salvation, for everlasting good news, for true
justice and mercy.

Give me insight and wisdom to know how to speak into
people's very hearts and minister true comfort based on
the promise of your kingdom. I want to see you magnified
now in people's eyes so they may rejoice in the day of your
coming rather than be filled with anxiety. Move me with your
Holy Spirit as you are also moved.

**In what way were the people Jesus saw like scattered
sheep? What direction did he believe they needed?**

# In Tune

I want you to understand what really matters, so that you may live
pure and blameless lives until the day of Christ's return.
PHILIPPIANS 1:10 NLT

I pray you would teach me, Father, what really matters to
you in this life as I eagerly await the return of my great
King. You desire purity; show me the way. You desire
blamelessness; teach me wisdom. Help me to live according
to your precepts and to take to heart the things you truly
value. This world has so much to offer to draw me after my
own comfort and joy, but not according to the joy you have
in store for me.

Transform my mind to be conformed to your will so I may
desire the things you desire which are also the things that
would be the most satisfying to my soul. I ask for your Holy
Spirit; may he share your wisdom with me and teach me the
ways that truly matter.

**What is the difference between a godly pleasure in this
life and one that leads to destruction?**

# SIT AND WAIT

Wait for the LORD;
be strong, and let your heart take courage;
wait for the LORD!
PSALM 27:14 NRSV

Oh Lord, I long for your kingdom. How long must I wait for you to fulfill your promises and restore me? How long must I be without my loved ones? When will you redeem me and raise me from the grave? I need your peace and your joy, oh Lord! Come and renew your creation, establish justice, rule in righteousness. Father, I wait on you. Renew my patience and perseverance. Though for you a hundred years are but a moment that passes, for me it feels so long. Renew my strength and courage to face the difficulties of life with confidence in your faithfulness.

Remind me daily that you can be trusted to do what you have said you would do. Though it feels like you are slow in fulfilling your commitment to renew the world, you are not slow but patiently drawing many others to yourself. Lord, I trust in you, I will endure with you, and I will wait for you!

**How do you wait for the Lord?**

# RELEASING KINDNESS

"Love your enemies, and do good, and lend, expecting nothing in return, and your reward will be great, and you will be sons of the Most High, for he is kind to the ungrateful and the evil."
LUKE 6:35 ESV

Father, help me to have the same heart you have for other people, to be giving without needing to be repaid for it. You give good things to all people. You provide food, you provide hospitable climates, you provide so many things we need even to those who hate you and spitefully act against you. You have set a day to exact justice from the wicked of the earth, but your heart is to see people live.

Help me to use restraint when dealing with people who abuse me. Give me your care and compassion for all people so I react well rather than reacting poorly to others. Increase my faith so I fully trust in your promise to avenge wrongs done to me and strengthen me to forgive others as I know I am forgiven in Jesus' name. I pray for your glory in the earth, oh Lord, in this age and in the world to come.

**Do you see God's kindness to his enemies serving a purpose?**

# Awe Inspired

"His mercy extends to those who fear him,
from generation to generation."
LUKE 1:50 NIV

Father, I stand in awe of you and of your great works.
Look at your creation: the lights in the sky, the landscapes
you have built, the artwork you have painted moment by
moment by your great, creative word. I magnify your name
because of what you have made! Yet you have done even
more. You have established your people in the earth, you
have set forth the hope of your restoration, and you have
made it known to all other people that your time is coming
to establish all good things and tear down all wickedness.
I delight in this goodness and wait for it with humble
anticipation.

Have mercy on me in this day, for you know where I
come from and of what things I have pursued, yet I have
turned to you and put my trust in your great work. May the
generations and people of the whole earth give honor to
your name because of your greatness!

**How does the fear of God lead to mercy?**

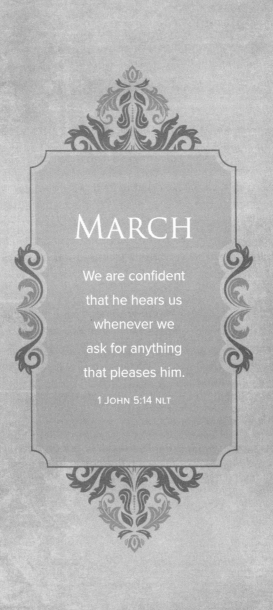

# MARCH

We are confident
that he hears us
whenever we
ask for anything
that pleases him.

1 JOHN 5:14 NLT

# CHANGE IS GOOD

Anyone who belongs to Christ has become a new person.
The old life is gone; a new life has begun!
2 CORINTHIANS 5:17 NLT

Oh Lord my God, we have waited for thousands of years to see your restoration fulfilled. Many people doubt the truth of your good news because of how long it has taken to bring it about. However, when I see the work of your Spirit in my own life, I know that you are still faithful to your promises and you are leading me toward the day of your promised glorification.

I am thankful to you that your good news has come to all nations to call us to prepare ourselves for your arrival, and I am grateful for your work in helping me to train myself through your Spirit and the circumstances of life which mold me into the character and image of your Son. Be glorified, oh Lord, and may justice and righteousness soon prevail on the earth.

**What do you think is Paul's reason to encourage us that the old life is gone when our circumstances so often declare it is not?**

# BUCKLING KNEES

Fear not, for I am with you;
be not dismayed, for I am your God;
I will strengthen you, I will help you,
I will uphold you with my righteous right hand.
ISAIAH 41:10 ESV

Oh Lord, I feel the weight of the world on my shoulders; I can't hold under the pressure. Help me to bear the burden. Strengthen me through your Holy Spirit to withstand the responsibilities you have placed on me. Give me the perspective to see the goal of this work and give me the encouragement I need to persevere. You have not given me more than I can handle with your assistance.

I trust you. You are a good King and you provide the resources I need to fulfill your assignment; I just request that you not forget me. Give me what I need so you may be glorified in the accomplishment of your established plans. I am yours to direct as you will, only do not let my foot stumble or my soul fall. Thank you for bearing with me, mighty God!

**What has God set you to do that provokes fear?**

# FAITH SPILLING OVER

"All things you ask in prayer, believing, you will receive."
MATTHEW 21:22 NASB

Lord, increase my faith and fill me with confidence that your promises to establish righteousness and restore goodness to the earth are certain. Turn my heart to these things and put my hope fully in the age to come where you will bring the reward to the righteous who persevere in living according to their trust in your good promises. Then, I will be pleased to ask you anything that brings you glory and sees your name exalted in the eyes of the nations, and you will be glad to fulfill my requests.

My hope is that the nations will turn back to you before the great and terrible day of your return so they may rejoice in the good you bring with you. Give me wise understanding of the ways I can help people recognize these truths and grant my requests that flow from this understanding. I love to see your name praised in righteousness and in truth. Be glorified in all the earth, my God.

**What is the goal of God giving you whatever you ask in faith?**

# Place for Me

"There are many rooms in my Father's house; I would not tell you this if it were not true. I am going there to prepare a place for you."
JOHN 14:2 NCV

Great God and Father, how magnificent it is that you have offered me a place in your righteous congregation, that you have desired to have me reside with you in the restored and glorified creation you are bringing to the earth. I am humbled that you would see me, a lowly man, and grant me the right to be called by your name. I am honored by your gift and excited to see the wonder of your fulfilled promises.

Come again soon and restore your creation, taking action to wipe clean the corruption that has marred your creation for so long. You have been merciful in withholding your wrath and judgment. Draw many people to your throne by your mercy, oh Lord. I long to find my place in your household when you have established it on the earth. Thank you for your good gifts.

**How long has God desired to give you a place in his presence?**

# MY MISTAKES

Though he fall, he shall not be cast headlong,
for the LORD upholds his hand.
PSALM 37:24 ESV

Father, sustain me and support me through the work of your Holy Spirit. This walk of faith is long and difficult, filled with many rough places and stumbling stones. Give me strength to withstand the obstacles and continue my walk on the other side. Forgive my stumbling and do not hold it against me but restore me and lift me back to my feet.

May my heart always seek after you and your glorification in all the earth. Though I falter at times, I am glad at the idea of you being exalted among the nations. Lift up my head and strengthen me to continue the walk. Oh God and King, be exalted and praised, for you and you alone deserve the adoration of the world.

**What does this promise from God mean to you, and how does it affect your walk?**

# Greater Meaning

"If a man has a hundred sheep but one of the sheep gets lost,
he will leave the other ninety-nine on the hill and
go to look for the lost sheep."
MATTHEW 18:12 NCV

I am thankful to you, Father, that you have such compassion
on the people you have created, and you have set in motion
your plans to draw people back to you. Your patience
to search out and prove the character of people from all
nations to include in your kingdom accentuates the wonder
of your diligence to establish your righteous kingdom.
Though all humanity has set itself against you and against
your wondrous plans, you have taken great measures to call
forth people from all nations to turn back to you, to swear
their allegiance to you, and to gain the opportunity to be
called according to your name.

Much like you did with Jesus the Messiah, you have been
willing to put your own special people through difficulty and
trial so that your good news would reach to the furthest
corners of the world. I am humbled at the way you have
reached forth your hand of friendship to me. May I be a
blessing to you in return.

**How have you been affected by God's tendency to do
what the Scripture above describes?**

# STRENGTH

I can do all this through him who gives me strength.
PHILIPPIANS 4:13 NIV

Lord, you are the source of my strength. I put my trust in you to take care of all my needs. You will not let me be put to shame, and even when my enemies think they have knocked me down, I know that you will vindicate your name when you restore me in the day of glory. You give me the peace and encouragement I need to withstand the circumstances of life that try to war against my hopefulness. You reinforce the truth of your faithfulness and remind me how good your promises are. Because of this, I can endure all sorts of difficulties.

Stay with me, oh Lord, and fill me with your Holy Spirit so I will be filled with the strength I need to complete the tasks you have set before me. I want to be joyfully welcomed into your wondrous kingdom.

**What does God's strength allow you to do?**

# Deepest Desire

"You will seek Me and find Me when you search for Me with all your heart."

JEREMIAH 29:13 NASB

Lord, how often I have sought you for my own desires and pleasures in this life, yet I have not found you. You have remained elusive to me in the days when I wanted you to grant me my wishes like a genie in a bottle. Instead, when I found myself at the end of my rope and needed you, you were there. You taught me your way and your patient endurance in anticipation of the day you have established by holy decree.

My heart is set on your promises and the restoration you have declared, and I seek your glory that you would be vindicated in the eyes of the nations as you see fit. I no longer hope in you for what you can give me now, but what you will do in the day of your glory. Be magnified in the earth, oh Lord, for the sake of the souls you desire to save.

**Do you remember times when you sought God but not with everything? How did that affect you?**

# CHILD OF THE KING

Your wife will be like a fruitful grapevine,
flourishing within your home.
Your children will be like vigorous young olive trees
as they sit around your table.
PSALM 128:3 NLT

I exalt your magnificent name, oh Lord my God. May worship flow from all regions of the earth toward your throne. How glorious the day will be when the waters flow abundantly in desert places and the trees produce ripe fruit for all to eat. In that day you will call all nations before you to celebrate, and we will come together to rejoice at the luscious feast you will have prepared.

You will be glorified in the eyes of the nations and your people will be approved in the assembly. I long for the day when the abundance of the products of your kingdom nourishes the world and everyone resides in the blessing of your good will.

**When you look at the circumstances of believers in so much of the world, why don't you see these promises fulfilled?**

# MY HELP

I look up to the mountains and hills, longing for God's help.
But then I realize that our true help and protection
come only from the Lord,
our Creator who made the heavens and the earth.
PSALM 121:1–2 TPT

Father, in this world we will have trouble. Even so, we know that you are coming again to rid the world of wickedness and establish blessing and righteousness in all nations, among all people. Strengthen me with that knowledge and let it propel me down the path of faith that builds character within me in preparation for the day when I will receive your deliverance from trouble.

You have made all things and rule over all; in patient restraint you delay justice for the sake of the wicked so they may find deliverance rather than destruction. In due time you will pour out your anger on the earth and wipe away injustice and wickedness in a flash. Only your people, who are called by your name, will stand in that day, and we will rejoice in the deliverance your works and wisdom have accomplished. For you I will wait, and to you I give my allegiance.

**What can you learn about how to act from God's slowness to deliver justice?**

# DRAWING ME BACK

May the Lord of peace himself give you peace at all times
in every way. The Lord be with you all.
2 THESSALONIANS 3:16 NIV

Father, fill me with the peace that comes from being assured
of your faithfulness and being certain of the goodness of
your promises. You have shown yourself to be faithful in
your dealings with humanity and you have remained true
to your promises. I know that you will restore all things by
your great power and sound wisdom, and you will establish
righteousness and justice in all the earth.

No longer will we need to be anxious about wicked rulers
and corrupt people who seek to rob and abuse others. No
longer will we need to be concerned about where to find
food or shelter. No longer will we need to be concerned
about hypocrisy and betrayal in our relationships, for you
are working all things together for the good of those who
are called according to your purpose, and you will raise us
up in the day of glory. I can rest easy in the knowledge of
your will.

**What is the source of God's peace and your joy?**

# THOUGH I FAIL

My flesh and my heart may fail,
but God is the strength of my heart
and my portion forever.
PSALM 73:26 NIV

God, when I consider the glory of your promises and
think about the result in store for those who despise your
instruction, I renew my devotion to your good kingdom and
persist in cultivating a righteous spirit within me. I look to
you to strengthen me with your own Spirit and draw me
down the path of righteousness. Fill me with the desire to
finish strong and not be distracted with what success others
seem to have in their lives.

I will be satisfied with your reward, oh Lord, and I glorify you.
You are supremely aware of the activity of people in the earth
and the ways they arrogantly seek prosperity in defiance
of your call to humility. Strengthen my desires and steel my
resolve to put my hope fully in your coming kingdom.

**What is it that causes your feet to stumble or your
heart to fail?**

# Too Much

"Give, and you will receive. You will be given much. Pressed down, shaken together, and running over, it will spill into your lap. The way you give to others is the way God will give to you."

LUKE 6:38 NCV

Father, every day I need a reminder of your great promises, of how your provision will exceed my imagination. Remind me of your desire to reward your people and see them prosper abundantly and how you will bless all nations through the restoration of the earth and reversal of the curse on the creation.

What reason have I to hold on to my possessions? You are generous in the way you treat me, and so I will give freely from my own resources—resources you have provided. You have given to me so I can share. Give me the wisdom and compassion to do so with ease and generosity. I trust in you, God. Because of the certainty of the hope you guarantee, I will pour forth your blessings to my neighbor.

**Why do you think God values a giver?**

# LAYING DOWN WEAPONS

"The LORD will fight for you, and you shall hold your peace."
EXODUS 14:14 NKJV

I trust in your righteousness and faithfulness, God, and I put my hope in your promises. You have established your people and will protect them by your sovereign power. I have no reason to seek my own protection because you have my back. I know that no matter what may happen to me, your hand will deal with my enemies, and I will be vindicated before them.

What have I to fear from anyone who may seek to destroy me? Your deliverance is soon at hand and you will raise up your righteous people. Instead, I will seek good for my enemies that they may learn your ways and turn from their animosity toward you so they may be saved in the day of your visitation. Thank you, Lord, for giving me assurance of your kindness. Be glorified in the congregation of the righteous.

**Why do you think it is important for believers to be careful about how they protect themselves?**

# THE SWEETEST FRUIT

The fruit of the Spirit is love, joy, peace, forbearance, kindness, goodness, faithfulness, gentleness and self-control. Against such things there is no law.
GALATIANS 5:22–23 NIV

My God, you have given generously of your Spirit to humanity; may I drink deeply from the fruit the Spirit produces. The fruit of the Spirit is your character, and you reveal yourself to me in these things. May my own character reflect the righteousness of your ways; I long to shine forth your goodness to the world. Fill me to overflowing with the hope of your salvation and grow the qualities of righteousness within me through every circumstance I face.

I trust in you, Lord, so give me the things I need that will please you. You created man in the beginning in your image and then filled him with your Spirit; I ask you to do it again. Shape me and mold me into the image of Jesus. As I reflect his character, reward me with the same gift you gave him— everlasting life.

**Why do you think these things are called the fruit of the Spirit? What do they represent?**

# Break My Heart

He was amazed to see that no one intervened to help the
oppressed. So he himself stepped in to save them
with his strong arm, and his justice sustained him.

ISAIAH 59:16 NLT

Father, I mourn for the lot of humanity in this age. How long
must we be subjected to the oppression of evil people?
When will you rescue us according to your righteousness
and love? How long must we see people starve because
of the policies of wicked rulers or see people exploited
because of the wicked acts of those who use them? Oh,
great God and King, turn your eye upon those who call on
your name in justice. Have mercy on me!

Father forgive me of my sins and do not let me be led astray
by the wickedness of my own heart. Give me the strength
to stand firm in righteousness before you and not to fall
into wickedness because of other people's actions. Call
all people to turn from their ways considering your coming
judgment and do not leave me to suffer too long. Help me
to speak peace and comfort to all who suffer at the hands of
the wicked and deliver me from this distress.

**What do you think you are called to do to help
the oppressed?**

# Your Motives

Am I now seeking the approval of man, or of God?
Or am I trying to please man? If I were still trying to please man,
I would not be a servant of Christ.

GALATIANS 1:10 ESV

Fill me with your Holy Spirit, God, so I will be moved according to the desires of your will. Show me the way to life everlasting and cause my steps to follow your path. Give me a singular focus on the goodness of your promised restoration so I am not turned to the right or the left by the distractions of life or by trying to satisfy the notions of the way humans think.

I do not wish to be turned away by seeking the approval of other people for that will not lead to righteousness in your kingdom. Shift my desires and cause the motivations of my life to be aimed at you. Make my way clear before you and I will serve you with all I am.

**What do you think is wrong with trying to please man?**

# LIVE ON PURPOSE

The LORD has made everything for its purpose,
even the wicked for the day of trouble.
PROVERBS 16:4 ESV

Oh great God and King of all the creation: you have set forth your creation in goodness and righteousness. Everything has its place and you did not put anything in place without purpose. You are a good Father who provides well for your children, and you have done so in a most miraculous way. I glorify you for your great works of old, and I magnify and praise you for your coming works of restoration.

Your creation will function just as you have decreed and designed, despite the attempts of your enemies to corrupt it. I ask for your Holy Spirit's wisdom to live according to your purposes in this life in anticipation of the restoration. Help me to practice now what you have purposed for then, so that in that day, I will be well prepared.

**What purpose does God have for you as an image bearer of Jesus? How can you best fulfill that today?**

# BEFORE I SPEAK

To watch over mouth and tongue
is to keep out of trouble.
PROVERBS 21:23 NRSV

Fill me with your Holy Spirit, Lord, to empower me with wisdom to consider my words carefully, humility to formulate them well, and self-control that keeps me from speaking rashly. May my words be a balm to others and not troublesome. May I be an encourager. Keep me from making extra trouble for myself with the words I speak, and let my words reflect your own. Watch over me to keep me steady and may the only trouble I face be for your name's sake.

I am willing to face trouble and difficulty for your sake, God, yet in that I need your provision to face it well. May your desires and passions shine through me and the words of my tongue speak from the source of that Spirit. Have mercy on me, Father, and grant my request. Keep me in your counsel until the day of your appearing.

**Does God promise you will avoid trouble if you follow his ways?**

# WHAT IS TRUE

It is the greatest joy of my life to hear that my children are
consistently living their lives in the ways of truth!

3 JOHN 1:4 TPT

Establish me in the truth of your Word, Lord, and draw
me to the full hope of your good news. Restore in me an
understanding of how temporary things in this life are and
refocus my attention on the permanence of the promises
you have established for the next life.

If it weren't for the grace of your Spirit, I would run after all
the temporary joys of this life. You sustain me by your Spirit
and your Word. Give me friends who also seek after your
coming promises and that fellowship will nourish my heart
until you come. How good and pleasant it is to live together
in the fellowship of the good news of Jesus!

**What are some things in your life that may be drawing
you away from consistently living for the hope of the
age to come?**

# LIGHT OF APPROVAL

Indeed, by faith our ancestors received approval.
HEBREWS 11:2 NRSV

Lord, you love the man who trusts you to fulfill your promises and who hopes in the establishment of your righteousness in the earth. You will establish him and set him in a place where he will never again be shaken by the world. You delight to do good to the man who delights in your instruction and whose will drives him toward the day of your exaltation. To him you will give great riches and exalt his position over the arrogant of the earth. I hear the testimony of the righteous who cry out even from the grave for the fulfillment of your great kingdom and the restoration of this creation that has been cursed.

I ask you to establish Jesus, your righteous King, in the throne you have promised to him. You have shown you approve of him when you resurrected him from crucifixion, and you have set him at your right hand until the day you intend to set up his throne in the earth. Make that day soon, Lord, and vindicate your name in all the earth.

**What do you think the ancestors did that resulted in approval?**

# CONTENTMENT

I am not saying this because I am in need, for I have learned to be
content whatever the circumstances.
PHILIPPIANS 4:11 NIV

Lord, I ask you for the instruction of your Spirit that I may
know the wisdom of contentment. Let me be fully engaged
in the plan you have established for the salvation of the
world and I will be able to accept any circumstance I
experience. The more I learn of your wonderful promises, of
your beautiful plans, the more I am strengthened to endure
even the most difficult times with the knowledge of what the
end of this path is.

My heart is filled with joy thinking about the goodness of
your kingdom and the righteousness of your governance
over creation. You are a worthy King and a gracious Father,
giving good things to your people. I am blessed to consider
that you have invited me to join you in your restoration of the
earth. How could the circumstances of this life get me down?

**What brings you contentment in your life?**

# No Need to Fear

I asked the LORD for help, and he answered me.
He saved me from all that I feared.
PSALM 34:4 NCV

Give me the strength to face life with full confidence, Lord,
for you will save me from all harm. Though I may fear attacks
from the enemy, you will restore me. What need I fear of
hunger, sickness, or trouble? I trust in you, oh Lord; do not
let me be put to shame before your enemies. Restore me
and provide for me according to your goodness and for your
name's sake.

Father, may your will be done in the earth and may your
justice put an end to the wickedness that abuses the world
and its people. May the arrogant be humbled so your mercy
may draw them to turn from their ways. Lord, stand for me in
my times of trouble and deliver me.

**What is a time when God came through to help you in
a circumstance you feared?**

# YOUR WILL

"Your kingdom come.
Your will be done,
On earth as it is in heaven."
MATTHEW 6:10 NASB

Oh Lord, I would that you would come soon. I eagerly long for your arrival and desperately desire your coming grace and peace. Release the curse the earth endures at your command and fill the earth with righteousness. Exalt your name in the eyes of the nations who have for so long ignored you or stood against you.

The kings of the earth will bow before you and submit to your will and peace and joy will go forth from your throne. The powers and principalities who have attempted to overthrow your will and ascend your throne will be judged and their false instruction will come to nothing in the day of your victory and restoration. Father, do not delay but come soon to fulfill your great and awesome promises to your people.

**When you consider the Lord's prayer, what imagery comes to mind regarding the fulfillment of this request?**

# NOT HELPLESS

When the righteous cry for help, the LORD hears
and delivers them out of all their troubles.
PSALM 34:17 ESV

Oh Father, in this world we will have trouble, but you have
provided a means to finally escape that trouble. Your
deliverance has been assured as we see through Jesus'
resurrection. You will certainly deliver me from the difficulties
and troubles of this life. Comfort me in the meantime with
this knowledge. I cry out to you for help, and if it be your will,
grant me deliverance even now. However, not my will but
yours be done.

Your restoration will put an end to all need, and you will
deliver us. Your provision in that day will be majestic and
beyond my ability to comprehend now. I trust in you that you
will help me and will not leave me to face alone the trials
that come. Give me your assistance, my God, for you are an
ever-present help in times of trouble.

**How would you reconcile the apparent contradiction
between the statement, "In this world you will have
trouble," and the encouragement, "Rejoice for I have
overcome the world"?**

# WITH JOY

Rejoice in the Lord always; again I will say, rejoice!
PHILIPPIANS 4:4 NASB

Mighty God, you are wondrous in all of your ways! How can I look at the magnificence of the creation you have set before us—the stars in the sky, the waters full of life, the beautiful landscapes and glorious sunsets—and not be filled with joy at the awesomeness of your works.

To think that such power and imagination is at work within me to mold me and train me to be a man worthy of your good gifts is amazing. To see how you have orchestrated history to bring the world to the point of decision and to vindicate your work, to vindicate your people, and to renew the majesty of the earth that you have sacrificed for my sake is beyond awesome. I am awed by the grandeur of your ways, Lord, and I love to consider the wonder of who you are.

**How would you describe the things for which God wants to be enjoyed?**

# Surrendered Mind

To set the mind on the flesh is death,
but to set the mind on the Spirit is life and peace.
ROMANS 8:6 NRSV

God, fix my eyes firmly on the fulfillment of your promised restoration and the coming of your kingdom. Help me keep from diverting to the things that satisfy my own desires. Instead, transform my mind to seek the desires you have set forth, to care for others, to draw people to turn from wickedness, to encourage the weak, and to wait patiently for the day of your return.

You have given me a course of action to pursue in the time I wait for you, so strengthen me to accomplish the tasks at hand and be faithful to your sovereign will. I want to serve rather than exalt myself. Give me the wisdom to live righteously before you and to stand strong against the temptation to defy you with the ways of this world.

**What do you think causes the things God has made to be good for us to become things of the flesh?**

# REPENTANCE MATTERS

"Repent of your sins and turn to God,
for the kingdom of Heaven is near."
MATTHEW 3:2 NLT

Lord, I ask you to daily renew the allegiance I give you
and your sovereign throne. Keep me from turning back to
worldly temptations that can so easily entangle me and draw
my focus away from the hope of the coming restoration.
Bind up my wandering desires with the increasing
knowledge of your good promises, for you will fulfill them in
good time.

Magnify your kingdom in my eyes so I may see it more
clearly in this age of darkness and distraction. Thank you,
my King, for your compassion and mercy to reach out to me
and offer forgiveness for my rebellion against you. Help me
to daily remember the favor you have extended to me.

**At its heart, what is repentance?**

# TEMPTED

Let no one say when he is tempted, "I am tempted by God";
for God cannot be tempted by evil,
nor does He Himself tempt anyone.

JAMES 1:13 NKJV

Guard my heart, oh Lord, by the power of your Holy Spirit. Give me the strength to put down the urges in my heart to satisfy my desires to not face difficulty. Help me to continually embrace your call to set aside the pursuit of satisfaction in this life for the much greater reward you will fulfill in your coming kingdom. Deliver me from the attacks of the enemy who tries to erode my faith in your good promises and divert my attention to the circumstances that bring fear and trepidation.

Fill my faith full to extinguish the enemy's attempts against my hope. You are my shield and deliverer which is why I trust you with my very life. Grant me your favor and I will stand in your presence in the assembly as we magnify your name.

**What is your best defense against the temptations you face?**

# NOT MY HOME

Stop imitating the ideals and opinions of the culture around you,
but be inwardly transformed by the Holy Spirit through
a total reformation of how you think. This will empower you
to discern God's will as you live a beautiful life, satisfying and
perfect in his eyes.

ROMANS 12:2 TPT

Lord, how majestic is your kingdom; how wonderful are the promises you have made to those who long for its arrival. Cause my thoughts and hopes to be fixated on receiving your prize and to be trained according to your wisdom to understand the times and to prepare for the task before me. Turn my attention away from this life and be ready to put aside my own personal satisfaction for the sake of pursuing your coming kingdom.

Help me to serve well and trust your work and plan completely. Be exalted in my eyes and show yourself faithful daily so I may be filled with the courage I need to continue in your righteous ways. Transform my thoughts and conform my character and desires to your own.

**How can you know what kind of lifestyle God values?**

# SELFISH AMBITION

"Whoever exalts himself will be humbled,
and whoever humbles himself will be exalted."
MATTHEW 23:12 ESV

My Lord, I want you to be glorified and exalted. Give me the
fortitude to stand firm. You are the King over all creation, for
you have made it, ordered, and preserved it. Your will be
done. I am nothing without you. You are the one who lifts up
or deposes leaders. Use me according to your will, my King,
and be magnified in the eyes of others for the tasks you set
before me. I trust in you both for provision to the task and
fulfillment of your promises to those who righteously seek
your glory.

Establish your will and kingdom in the earth as you have
declared and receive the praise and worship due your
glorious name. I choose to give you my allegiance and to
defer to your majesty; I no longer desire to exalt myself.
Thank you for your generous mercy to me though I have
been a sinner before you. I know my ways have not always
sought your glory. Have your way in me, majestic Lord.

**What have you been called to give up for the sake
of humility?**

# APRIL

The earnest prayer
of a righteous person
has great power and
produces wonderful
results.

JAMES 5:16 NLT

# No Criticism

Keep a good conscience so that in the thing
in which you are slandered, those who revile
your good behavior in Christ will be put to shame.
1 PETER 3:16 NASB

Father, I know that your good promises will be established in the earth, and your name will be lifted high. You will be exalted in all your ways, and the people of the earth will bow down to you in awe. You will lift your faithful servants up before all people and their works will be exalted before them, and they will give glory to you for your righteous judgment. No longer will your loved ones be abused or insulted because of the ways you have taught them.

In your day of judgment, all will be revealed, and the futility of the world's wisdom will be put on full display. Be magnified, God, and come quickly to deliver your people. May your righteousness be revealed in glory!

**Why do you think God permits his people to be mistreated and slandered?**

# PRONE TO WANDER

LORD, I know that people's lives are not their own;
it is not for them to direct their steps.
JEREMIAH 10:23 NIV

Oh Lord my God, your ways are righteous and good; you have established the way that is right and have given your instruction as to the direction of that path. You are King of all. Why do I plan in vain the steps of my life before you as if you would be satisfied with any path I might choose? Instead, may your Holy Spirit direct me and instruct me in the path to travel. The path is rough and unpaved—the road less traveled in the earth—yet you also strengthen me to keep my way faithful.

According to your grace, make me righteous in your sight so that you may raise me up in the last day and I may live with you in righteousness forever. You are our Creator and King, and accordingly, my life belongs to you. Have your way in me and be glorified.

**How important is it to learn the lesson that your life is not your own to direct? How deep does this issue go?**

# You Are Perfect

As for God, His way is perfect;
The word of the LORD is proven;
He is a shield to all who trust in Him.
PSALM 18:30 NKJV

Oh Lord, you are faithful and true in all your ways, and you can be trusted in all things you have declared. Those who put their hope in you will not be put to shame, but you will protect them from all the arrows of the enemy. You are faithful to deliver them to the day of your salvation. You have proven yourself true in your dealings with humanity, and your faithfulness to your people has been shown repeatedly, both for their blessing and their discipline.

I can rest assured that you will deliver on all your promises of restoration and blessing in the day of your glory. I glorify and magnify your holy name because of your great works of righteousness.

**Do you think there are there specific characteristics about God that make him perfect or is perfection simply one of his characteristics?**

# SOURCE OF HOPE

I pray that God, the source of hope, will fill you completely with joy and peace because you trust in him. Then you will overflow with confident hope through the power of the Holy Spirit.
ROMANS 15:13 NLT

Oh Lord, your ways are marvelous, and you are to be glorified for your great works. You have shown yourself faithful to your promises and we can have great hope because of your faithfulness and lovingkindness. How magnificent are your promises yet to be fulfilled? They make your former works look small in comparison. How wonderful it is to be able to look forward to them.

Considering your faithfulness and how much better your fulfilled promises will be than anything we encounter in this life; my heart is put at ease and I am overjoyed because of your good news. May others be drawn to the hope of your restoration and put their trust in you as well. May the earth be filled with the glory of your works as we anticipate the culmination of the age.

**God is the source of hope, but what about him gives you reason to hope?**

# DESIRING HUMILITY

The reward for humility and fear of the LORD
is riches and honor and life.
PROVERBS 22:4 ESV

Throughout your Word you declare that you will exalt the humble but lay the proud and arrogant low. Teach me to humble myself before you, Lord. You are certainly the highest of Kings and the mightiest of all Lords, yet you are meek in the way you express it, exhibiting patience rather than moving swiftly, and so I sometimes forget your great majesty.

Remind me daily of the magnificence of your throne so I will bow before your majesty. I know my place as your servant; secure this knowledge in the depths of my heart and cause me to walk before you in humility and deference. You are my great King and glorious God. I exalt your wonderful name.

**When do you think the humble receive their reward?**

# CANNOT BE LOST

Every valley shall be raised up,
every mountain and hill made low;
the rough ground shall become level,
the rugged places a plain.
ISAIAH 40:4 NIV

Lord, you will never abandon your people who call upon you in humility and righteousness. You go to the ends of the earth to find them and to restore them according to your faithful Word. You shake the foundations of the world, the nations and all they trust in, to pave a righteous path for your people to travel.

Uphold me, my God, with your righteousness and do not let me fall as you shake the high places of the earth. As the systems of the world falter before your testing, fill me with your Spirit and desires so I do not waver in my devotion to your coming kingdom. Sustain me and preserve me in the midst of trial and difficulty. Thank you for your patient endurance and faithful support. I trust in you.

**What are some things that God has been shaking in your life to bring forth good for you?**

# Renew My Mind

Let the Spirit renew your thoughts and attitudes.
EPHESIANS 4:23 NLT

Renew my innermost thoughts and dreams, oh Lord, and conform them to your own. According to your Holy Spirit, make your desires and motivations my own. Set my hopes on everlasting life in the righteous kingdom you have promised to your people. Turn my thoughts away from satisfaction in this life to seek the satisfaction that your restoration will bring.

I know that I will be filled with the patience you also have to wait and seek the salvation of others rather than revenge. When you build in me the thoughts, desires, and attitudes you desire, then I will stand firmly for your good news and rejoice that it is sent forth. Thank you for giving me the gifts of your instruction and your Spirit to cause me to joyfully conform my life to your righteousness.

**What is the renewal of your thoughts and attitudes?**

# Made to Be

Since we have gifts that differ according to the grace given to us,
each of us is to exercise them accordingly.
ROMANS 12:6 NASB

Teach me to use my talents and skills in a way to exalt your
name, God. I want to be a blessing to you in my actions and
a good steward of the resources you have provided me. For
some reason, it often seems easy to use the talents you've
given for corrupted ways, to seek my exaltation and to
insulate myself from the suffering that can help build godly
character. Use my talents for your glory. I know it is often
difficult to do. I know you have made me to glorify your
name and promote the good news of your coming kingdom,
and you have made it so I can work with others to produce a
beautiful testimony in your name.

Give me wisdom and activate my imagination to inspire
me and give my will the strength it needs to step out and
exercise the gifts you have produced in me. I thank you for
your generosity and for trusting me with your resources.
May they produce an abundant harvest for your kingdom in
the restoration of all things.

**Has God given you a gift that seems difficult to get
traction in exercising for his glory?**

# WISE ENOUGH

If any of you is lacking in wisdom, ask God, who gives to all generously and ungrudgingly, and it will be given you.
JAMES 1:5 NRSV

Father, I marvel at the magnitude of your wisdom and the way you have established the workings of the world. Your plans are manifold in their scope, and they do not accomplish mere simple tasks. Teach me your wisdom and help me to understand your ways. I desire to be versed in the nature of your work in the world and the way you are piloting the course of events to land at the day of your great glory. Help me to follow your path according to your great wisdom and not to follow my own understanding.

In my own understanding, I would not be nearly as patient and compassionate as you have been. Your wisdom will teach me the path of righteousness which leads to receiving the prize of my faith. Thank you for your wisdom that is the blueprint for how to live according to your desired purposes and within your ordained created order. You willingly and joyfully give wisdom to all who ask you for it. You are gracious to me. I will bless your righteous name.

**What do you think the purpose of wisdom is?**

# WILLING SUBMISSION

Obey your leaders and act under their authority. They are watching over you, because they are responsible for your souls. Obey them so that they will do this work with joy, not sadness. It will not help you to make their work hard.

HEBREWS 13:17 NCV

Father, you established a governmental hierarchy over your creation. You set up rulers and powers and, last of all, you gave humanity authority over the earth. Each group of people and nation has an established governing authority acting according to the divine mandate you have established.

I submit myself to your will and to the governing authorities you have established, knowing full well that many of them do not act in submission to your sovereignty. Grant them wisdom, in as much as they will use it, and help them to realize their true responsibility. May they rule righteously and for the good of those whom they govern, not attempting to use the position you have given them for selfish gain. Teach our government leaders the true nature of servant leadership and remind them of their accountability to you.

**How difficult do you find it to submit to the governing authorities as if they were God's agents?**

# SELF-DISCIPLINE

As for us, we have all of these great witnesses who encircle us like clouds. So we must let go of every wound that has pierced us and the sin we so easily fall into. Then we will be able to run life's marathon race with passion and determination, for the path has been already marked out before us.

HEBREWS 12:1 TPT

Father, you have been gracious and generous to me in my life. You have offered me a place in your righteous kingdom and have extended your peace to me. You have provided for my needs and often given me more than I need. The grace of your instruction is so beneficial to me. You have recorded the faithful acts of those who have put their trust in you, but you have also left the encouragement of recording so many of their failings to let me know that we all fail at times.

You are faithful to help me and set me on the path when I turn from my faulty ways. I will trust in your Word and the encouragement it provides, submitting to the discipline you provide to produce self-control in me. Your Word shines so much light on the path you have set before me; give me the wisdom to understand your instruction. Thank you for your precious Word and Spirit guiding me in the path that leads to righteousness and the reward of everlasting life.

**Whose example encourages you to faithfully run this race of faith?**

# Real Future

Come now, you who say, "Today or tomorrow we will go to such and such a town and spend a year there, doing business and making money." Yet you do not even know what tomorrow will bring. What is your life? For you are a mist that appears for a little while and then vanishes. Instead you ought to say, "If the LORD wishes, we will live and do this or that."

JAMES 4:13–15 NRSV

Your lovingkindness and faithfulness are greater than I could imagine, God, and I magnify your name before people because of your great mercy. Thank you for the promise you have made, giving it even to Adam and Eve, to restore the creation and reverse the curse of death. Your message was that this life is temporary and will not last forever. Whatever I have in this life, good or bad, is but a shadow or a wispy vapor that essentially disappears. However, you have plans to expand blessing and extend life.

You are the good God who establishes my steps regardless of my plans. You work all things together to produce a righteous temperament within me so you can give me the reward you desire to impart. I will submit to your governance in this life, knowing that you are the true and great King. Guide me in your wisdom, and I will conduct the business of life in the instruction of your Spirit.

**Who holds the authority in this life?**

# Present

No one has ever seen God. But if we love each other, God lives in us, and his love is brought to full expression in us.
1 JOHN 4:12 NLT

Father, fill me with your wondrous heart of compassion and care for people, so I may testify to your goodness among the nations. Help me to express true affection for the assembly of believers and dedicate myself to serving them in training and encouragement to walk this faith life together. It is so much more enjoyable and exciting to walk down a path with a group of likeminded people who love and honor each other, encourage each other, enjoy the adventure, and have fun together. Even more so is the support one can gain from his brothers in arms as they each face trials and struggles together.

May the world get a taste of your glory through the camaraderie of fellow believers walking together in peace and love. Though many will despise what they see, I trust you to touch many people with the expression of compassion and generosity and draw them to turn to your promised kingdom.

**How can you show greater love and care to your fellow Christians?**

# Still Promised

"For I know the plans I have for you," declares the LORD,
"plans to prosper you and not to harm you, plans to
give you hope and a future."
JEREMIAH 29:11 NIV

Thank you for your amazing promises of life and fullness,
great God and King. You honor me and I am humbled for I
know that I am not worthy to receive the gifts you anticipate
handing out. Only by your strength and training will I be able
to sustain to the end of this path, yet that is all part of your
good plans for me, to transform and mold my corrupted
intentions according to the goodness of your Spirit.

Father, I ask you to be diligent to train me and to spur
me along the path of your righteousness, teaching me to
understand the nature of your plan. I greatly cheer for the
things you have in store, eagerly anticipating the day you
finally reveal them to the world. May it be that many people
would turn their hearts toward you, devote themselves to
you, and be lifted up as well when you come. May your
house be filled with those who love your ways.

**Can a plan to do good include times of difficulty
along the path?**

# JEALOUSY

Wrath is fierce and anger is a flood,
But who can stand before jealousy?
PROVERBS 27:4 NASB

God, you are majestic above all else and worthy to be praised. You are to be exalted and honored in all the earth. Instead, we have given our allegiance to other gods, mere creatures you have made, and because of it, we have corrupted your creation. We have cultivated wickedness and governed according to earthly wisdom. You zealously love your creation and the people you have made and you jealously seek the honor due your name. Who will be able to stand in the day of your judgment? We have polluted your good world with our selfishness and idolatry, and your jealousy burns because of this abuse of our position and power.

Father, I am so thankful for your great mercy and patient endurance to afford me the opportunity to turn back to you and to rightly place my devotion before you. Thank you for your forgiveness.

**Do you think of jealousy as a wicked thing? When is it good?**

# My
# Reconciliation

If while we were enemies we were reconciled to God
by the death of his Son, much more, now that we are reconciled,
shall we be saved by his life.

ROMANS 5:10 ESV

How beautiful your plans are to me, my great God and King, for you have orchestrated such an elaborate plan to preserve your people and extend the offer of peace to the nations. I am humbled and overwhelmed with the favor you have shown to me though I have given you no reason to do so. The means by which you have created a plan that calls, purifies, reconciles, builds character, and tests the nature of humanity accomplishing all together is mind-boggling to me.

Your ways are so much more glorious than my own and your wisdom to be envied. Father, I ask you to teach me your ways according to your instruction; show me your righteous paths in the power of the Holy Spirit. You have called me even though I have rebelled against you. You have made me one of your own. May you receive all the praise due your name for you are amazing.

**What do you think the purpose of reconciliation is?**

# BEAUTY IN PAIN

"In the same way I will not cause pain
without allowing something new to be born," says the LORD.
"If I cause you the pain, I will not stop you from giving birth
to your new nation," says your God.

ISAIAH 66:9 NCV

Lord, I am overwhelmed that you have reached out to me
to offer me salvation. In this life there is much pain and trial.
Purging wickedness from myself hurts and often leads to
circumstances I would not choose for myself. God, you have
not left me to face these circumstances in futility, but you are
working to produce in me godly character and, in the end,
the reward of everlasting life.

Search me and know me, oh Lord, purge me and bring forth
the righteous man you have desired for ages. I will exalt
you in the midst of the congregation of righteous nations
because you have been faithful to bring forth the beauty of
your promised restoration.

**Do you find that you often try to avoid the painful
times in your life?**

# Already Won

"The LORD your God is the one who goes with you to fight for you against your enemies to give you victory."

DEUTERONOMY 20:4 NIV

Oh conquering King, you rule in righteousness and fullness over all that your hands have made. You are gracious and you have given even your enemies some leeway to rule according to their own desires, to a point. But you have full power and sovereignty over all the earth. Lord, rise up and fulfill the promises you have established by your just decree generations ago.

You are the King who will lead into the battle and restore the creation according to your powerful Word. We magnify you and join with the hosts of heaven in praising you for your glorious work. Your enemies think they can scheme to overthrow your decrees and seize power for themselves, but your victory is already assured. We long for the day when you bring your promises to completion.

**When the enemies of God seem to gain small victories in your day-to-day life, what gives you hope?**

# CARRYING ENOUGH

"What does it profit them if they gain the whole world,
but lose or forfeit themselves?"
LUKE 9:25 NRSV

So often, God, I am distracted by the things of the world because I forget the wonder of the life to come. Continually remind me that you will reward the righteous, but that those who seek their reward in this life will receive nothing more in the age to come. Remind me that I can trade my place in your coming kingdom for the fleeting prizes of this life, or I can choose to persist in following you and receive my prize in your timing.

Lord, the evil that people do to each other is so often rooted in the desire to improve their own lot in this life. We abuse others, oppress others, and overlook them on our way to fulfilling our own desires. Help me to wait on you to fulfill me and to give me my needs and your desires. I will trust you.

**How does gaining good things in this life place you in jeopardy of losing your place in the next life?**

# DEFEAT IS IMPOSSIBLE

You will prosper, if you take care to fulfill the statutes and
judgments with which the LORD charged Moses concerning Israel.
Be strong and of good courage; do not fear nor be dismayed.

1 CHRONICLES 22:13 NKJV

Gracious God, how thankful I am that you have given me
your Word that can order my steps and redirect my choices.
How kind you have been to provide a book of instruction to
lead me into the truth of your work in the world. You have
led your people out of captivity to become the light of all
nations and by the light you have provided them, you draw
me close to your good news.

Strengthen my heart to stand against the temptations that
desire to lead me away from your good promises. As I follow
your Word and obey your commands, I will never need to
be afraid of what the future has in store, for you will uphold
the righteous by your right hand and fulfill your promises to
exalt those who humble themselves in obedience to your
commands.

**What does God's Word provide as the means of living
free from fear?**

# As I Know It

This world and its desires are in the process of passing away, but those who love to do the will of God live forever.

1 JOHN 2:17 TPT

Father, how am I to imagine the wonder of the renewed creation you have promised to bring to pass? My experience is so different from your promises that they boggle my imagination. Give me understanding according to your Holy Spirit so I may consider its wonder. Strengthen me in your wisdom so I may stand firm to receive the prize. May your teaching encourage me to persevere in the face of trouble and difficulty that is so common in this life.

I will put my hope in you to fulfill your promises and restore the earth as you have said because your Spirit will confirm the wisdom of putting my trust in you. Daily renew my commitment to your sovereign will, for I would enter your righteousness and be nourished by your promises. By your will, I will stand in opposition to the call of the world.

**What are some things that defy your imagination that you look forward to receiving in the age to come?**

# MATCHING WISDOM

"With God are wisdom and might;
he has counsel and understanding."
JOB 12:13 ESV

Magnificent Father, I desire that you be praised for the incomparability of your wisdom. You are wondrous in the paths you have devised and the plans you have conceived. They are unapproachable in their creativity and magnificence and unassailable in their effectiveness. Though you disclose your plans to your enemies, they are still unable to resist them. Every act they take in rebellion against you further solidifies the certainty that your plans will succeed.

You are without equal in all the creation and no one can resist the implementation of your plans. If I submit to them, you accept me as a son and purify my way. Your ways are amazing, my Lord, and I give my honor and praise to you. May your name be exalted among all the nations and in the mouths of all the leaders of the earth.

**What do you think makes God's wisdom so miraculous?**

# EACH HOLY ACT

Pursue peace with everyone, and the holiness
without which no one will see the Lord.
HEBREWS 12:14 NRSV

Oh Father, that the world would know true peace; that war
and violence would cease to be such a mainstay of human
interaction. It seems unimaginable, yet I long for it. Develop
the ability to defer my own satisfaction and the defense of
my own rights and justice. Teach me to control my temper
and to see with the eyes you use to see others. Remind
me of the selfishness I harbor so that I may forgive the
selfishness of others; in this way I will be slow to judge.

I thank you for the confidence you give me regarding your
righteous promises and the character you are building in
me. Let that confidence translate into the ability to refrain
from demanding my own way. Help me to mimic your
restraint in my dealings with others so that peace may be
the result, and perhaps they may be drawn to your nature.

**What do you think is the source of the aggression and
violence the world experiences?**

# IT WILL BE DONE

I also persevered in the work on this wall, and we acquired no
land, and all my servants were gathered there for the work.

NEHEMIAH 5:16 ESV

I am confident in your faithful kindness to the earth, God,
and how wonderfully you will reward those who diligently
seek your kingdom. I am excited to see the work you will
do, and how you will restore the earth. You will be praised
above all creatures, as is right, and your glory will go forth
from the temple you restore. Your house will be a place for
all nations to gather and glorify you and to receive from you
the abundant provisions you have longed to give.

You have created humanity on the earth to be your
righteous governors and to glorify you in the earth, and
many people from all nations will be pleased to exalt your
name. Thank you for offering me a place at your feast and
help me to prepare for it.

**What do you look most forward to experiencing
in eternity?**

# BORN OF PAIN

"This is My commandment, that you love one another,
just as I have loved you."
JOHN 15:12 NASB

Father, give me the grace to love my neighbors and friends with the love Jesus exemplified. Help me to care for those who need your good news, to righteously confront those who need repentance, to hold fast to those who have entrusted themselves to you. Give me the strength and the wisdom to live responsibly and joyfully with those who also hope in you and wish to live out their lives in this age with longing anticipation of your coming.

Help me to understand your gracious love in truth and minimize my own interpretation of it, so others may experience your love and not my flawed affection. Father, help me to truly love others the way Jesus loved them.

**When you look at the ways Jesus interacted with people, what are some differences between the way he showed love and the way you think love is shown?**

# BEAUTIFUL REFLECTION

One thing I ask from the LORD, this only do I seek:
that I may dwell in the house of the LORD all the days of my life,
to gaze on the beauty of the LORD and to seek him in his temple.
PSALM 27:4 NIV

How majestic it is to consider you and the wonder of your love, your care, and your power, oh Lord my God. If only I would remember how much better it is to be found in your presence than any other thing this world has to offer. You have created the earth to be a provision for me and a place where we can come together in fellowship, yet I so often seek after things that are much less satisfying. Expand my hope and desire for you. Help me to wait patiently for you, and, rather than getting distracted by light and momentary pleasures, keep whetting my appetite for you.

May I daily consider your goodness; may I daily consider the joy of living in a world you have glorified and in which I may find your presence. How much better it will be fellowship with you in a world wholly devoted to your glory. Be exalted, oh my God, in fullness of word and deed.

**What do you think makes dwelling close to God such a thing to desire that you might forsake everything else?**

# My Safety

They will not be disgraced in hard times;
even in famine they will have more than enough.
PSALM 37:19 NLT

Uphold me, God, in difficult times and I will glorify you. You stand with the righteous and those who trust you rather than their own strength. I put my hope in you and seek to follow the path you have set for me. Strengthen me and sustain me. In your mercy and favor, provide for my needs forever and ever. I give you my devotion and offer you my skill to do as you command me and to go where you send me. I am your devoted servant. I owe you more than I can give.

Though your enemies have sought to destroy me in this life, I will not be put to shame before you because I trust you for my good and I seek your kingdom and righteousness. I know that you will establish me in the day of your coming so I will have an everlasting possession in your kingdom because you are faithful to all who trust in you. I give you glory and honor, God, and thank you for your provision.

**Why do you think we see believers going hungry and apparently disgraced in times of trouble?**

# ACCEPT THE WAITING

"Then you will call upon Me and go and pray to Me,
and I will listen to you."
JEREMIAH 29:12 NKJV

Lord my God, hear my requests for I turn my face to you
and seek the glory of your kingdom. Forgive me the error
of my ways and have mercy on the evil I have committed
in your sight. I am at your mercy, and I put myself in your
hands since I know you are a merciful King. Hear my plea
for reconciliation. I trust that you are a good God who does
not desire to see the wicked destroyed but come to peace
with you. I know that you will not ignore the requests of the
humble, the requests of those who bow themselves in honor
before your sovereign authority.

I exalt you, my God, for I am nothing but a servant before
you. Hear me and I will be satisfied. Give heed to my
request for mercy and I will be content. You are the great
and marvelous God, the King over all creation, and I honor
you. Thank you for your good actions toward your
humble servant.

**What precedes God's declaration in Jeremiah 29:12?**

# THANKFUL IN TRIALS

My brothers and sisters, whenever you face trials of any kind,
consider it nothing but joy, because you know that the testing of
your faith produces endurance; and let endurance have its full
effect, so that you may be mature and complete,
lacking in nothing.

JAMES 1:2–4 NRSV

Father, I am glad that you have chosen to test me and train
me in the fear and admonition of the Lord and that you have
chosen to discipline me and to mold me into the image of
your faithful Son, Jesus. I know the effects of solid training
and the way the results produce fruitfulness. Though the
experience at the time can be difficult, and the aftereffects
leave me sore, the result in my life is good and pleasing.

I am grateful to you for your persistence in discipline
because it means you have not given up on me even though
I sometimes resist the training you offer and try to run from
the exercises you put me through. You are compassionate
and patient with me and your goodness will produce good
fruit. I am glad to have your invitation to join with your
people in restoration, and humbled that you would consider
me for your service.

**Do you consider trials a gift from God to be embraced
or something to be avoided and ended quickly?**

# WHERE YOU ARE

"Where two or three are gathered in my name,
there am I among them."
MATTHEW 18:20 ESV

How awesome it is for me to gather with others who have
given themselves to your kingdom. You have known that it
was not good for us to be alone since the very beginning, so
you have called out many who encourage each other and
lift each other's spirits. We are glad to be called according
to your name. Exalt your name in our assemblies. May the
nations see your goodness and favor in our meetings and
be enticed to turn to you.

Father, may faith in you be a light to those who reside in the
dark. Work your miracles in the sight of the nations to teach
them the truth of your Word. May our love one for each
other testify to your love for us. I am glad and humbled to be
a part of your family.

**How do you think God is found in an assembly
together with the congregants?**

# MAY

I pray that your hearts will
be flooded with light so
that you can understand
the confident hope he
has given to those he
called—his holy people
who are his rich and
glorious inheritance.

EPHESIANS 1:18 NLT

# A Glimpse

Surely there is a future,
And your hope will not be cut off.
PROVERBS 23:18 NASB

Father, I need you to show me a sign of your
trustworthiness. I believe in your faithfulness and goodness,
yet I am also weak and need your encouragement. May your
Spirit give me a gift to help me remain faithful to the path of
righteousness. Remind me of your goodness; show me that
your promises are trustworthy and true. May my heart cease
being troubled in the midst of the difficulties of life.

I face many trials and struggles, God, just as your Son
experienced in his time. Sustain me with the same Spirit you
sustained him, and mold me into an even more accurate
representation of the man you have desired since the
creation of the world. Cure me with the fires of trials, but do
not forget my wayward heart and strengthen it amid the fire.

**What purpose do you think God's miraculous works
serve in your daily life?**

# CAPTIVES SET FREE

We have freedom now, because Christ made us free. So stand strong. Do not change and go back into the slavery of the law.
GALATIANS 5:1 NCV

I thank you, Father, for providing a way of escape from captivity to sin and its consequence, death. You have made a way for me to be freed from the punishment you have established for those who violate your righteous decrees. Thank you for your great mercy and desire to see people saved from wrath rather than destroyed.

Give me the strength I need to reside in your will and to persevere in living righteously before you. Change my heart so I live according to your precepts out of love and allegiance to you rather than out of obligation. May my desires be shifted and aligned with your will. Be glorified, oh great and forgiving God! May your ways be exalted in the earth and your majesty be known among all nations.

**What do you think the difference is between the call to live righteously before God and the warning not to become enslaved to the law?**

# ALL I CARRY

"The foreigner residing among you must be treated as your native-born. Love them as yourself, for you were foreigners in Egypt. I am the LORD your God."

LEVITICUS 19:34 NIV

Father, you have treated me with great kindness and have accepted me even though I was an enemy to you. You have done good things for me and provided for my needs. Help me to treat others in the same way. Help me to remember my lowly position and be gracious to others who are different than me. Help me to share with other people the good news you have shared with me and desire to see all people come to give their allegiance to your throne.

I desire to be a part of your people living and working in our coming kingdom for your glory and the benefit of all the earth. Help me to live in harmony with others because of the greatness of your name and the sovereignty of your throne. Be exalted my God and King.

**What things challenge you to treat people of different cultures with the same love as yourself?**

# ENEMIES WILL SEE

"Blessed are those who are persecuted for righteousness' sake,
for theirs is the kingdom of heaven."
MATTHEW 5:10 NKJV

Father, I pray that your enemies will see your goodness and
be inspired to turn from their ways. Even as they persecute
the righteous, may our mercy and grace in the experience
cause them to seek what causes our reactions, and may
they find your Holy Spirit as the cause. Help me put my full
trust in you, so I may react with appropriate grace in the time
of persecution.

Lord, you know my heart, that I desire justice and want to
see victimizers face their appropriate retribution, yet while
I share that in common with you, I need your help to mimic
your desire to see the wicked repent and be saved. Fill
me with this compassion and with greater faith in your day.
Justice will be done in its appropriate time. May you be
glorified both for your mercy and your justice.

**How does the good news of the gospel impact your
attitude toward those who mistreat others?**

# WITHIN THE WALLS

"Peace be within your walls,
and security within your towers."
PSALM 122:7 NRSV

Oh Lord my God, watch over me and my family. I put my trust and hope in you and ask for your peace and provision. You have promised to care for me as I devote myself to you, and I humble myself in acceptance of your Word. I bow my will to yours as I no longer need to fight for my own provision and safety. Moreover, I can also trust that even if I face trouble and danger in this life, your true promises assure me that you will care for me in eternity.

Father, you know how you made me as a man and the things I am compelled to do as part of my nature, the very things you designed in me. Give me the capacity to set those things aside in deference to your plans to bring forgiveness to the world.

**Have you experienced times in life when you have not felt you had peace and security? What did you do in those times to remain hopeful.**

# INSIDE OUT

"Don't judge by his appearance or height, for I have rejected him.
The LORD doesn't see things the way you see them. People judge
by outward appearance, but the LORD looks at the heart."

1 SAMUEL 16:7 NLT

Father, you have known the heart of men since the day you
established us on the face of the earth. You made us in your
image and created us to reflect yourself. You know me to
the very depths of my motivations. Cleanse me according to
your desire and through the work of your Spirit within me.
Give me the desires that align with your work. May not only
my works but my whole being be devoted to you.

Mold me as a man to reflect you with clarity and distinction.
May I not be a hazy image of the glorious King of the
universe. Help me to be wise and discerning in evaluating
people's ways in the earth. I want to remain faithful in my
word and deed before you until the day we meet face
to face.

**What are some ways that you need Jesus to help you
become a true reflection of God's character?**

# WHEN WE DOUBT

Keep being compassionate to those who still have doubts.
JUDE 1:22 TPT

My Lord, I thank you for your great compassion and mercy to people who love and follow you yet still struggle with depth in their faith. You are good to sustain me. I think of Jesus' disciples whom he consistently accused of having little faith, and in the time of trial they all abandoned him. Father, you give me grace because I am not yet perfect in all my understanding or the choices I make. They may not always reflect a full belief in your return, yet you strive with me and patiently guide and direct me along the path you have set before me.

I ask for your continued grace to show me your ways and fill me with the will to follow your desires. Restore me when I deviate from your good plan and righteous commands.

**What do doubts about God's plans and will cause within you?**

# Fear No Evil

Even though I walk through the valley of the shadow of death,
I fear no evil, for You are with me;
Your rod and Your staff, they comfort me.

PSALM 23:4 NASB

Lord my God, what do I have to fear of evil since you have promised me life everlasting? You are faithful to fulfill your great promises and to establish me according to your desire to see the wicked restored and the righteous rewarded. I have placed my trust in you and put my hope in your promises, so I entrust my life to your guidance and direction.

Do not let me be put to shame. Exalt your name in the earth, and specifically in my own life, and you will give me the courage and strength to endure any attack of the enemy. I will walk through the trials and will come through them to receive the reward you have promised me. Keep me on your straightened path, my God, and let me know you accept me as a son.

**What reason might some people have to fear evil? When would such a fear make sense?**

# My Inspiration

All Scripture is given by inspiration of God,
and is profitable for doctrine, for reproof,
for correction, for instruction in righteousness.
2 TIMOTHY 3:16 NKJV

God, you have inspired me and triggered my imagination!
When I consider your works from the beginning of creation,
the way you have delivered your people, the way you have
set about spreading the good news, and the way you have
orchestrated world events to create a means of purifying
your servants, I am filled with awe and wonder.

When I see the creation itself, in all its wonder and majesty,
the vibrancy of color and the intricacy of systems of life, I
marvel at this God who will raise the dead to life and sustain
them for everlasting ages. You are magnificent in your ways,
oh Lord, and your Scriptures guide and direct our steps
toward you.

**What does God hope to inspire in you?**

# ALL I AM

"Love the LORD your God with all your heart,
all your soul, and all your strength."
DEUTERONOMY 6:5 NCV

Lord, I give myself to you again this day. Take me as your own and set me upon the path you desire for me. As a man of action, set me to work in your service. Fill me with your Spirit so I do not seek my own glory but submit in humility to your plans. Help me to be diligent in all you give me to do and teach me mercy in my interactions with other people.

I set aside my desire to accrue power and position. I want to use my resources for the benefit of others, so that in the day of your glory more people will experience your goodness because of the way you have blessed them through me. Grant me to follow in your steps, oh Lord, and honor you in all I do.

**How do you love God with all your heart, soul, and strength?**

# YOU GET ME

We do not have a high priest who is unable to empathize with our weaknesses, but we have one who has been tempted in every way, just as we are—yet he did not sin.
HEBREWS 4:15 NIV

Father, you have created me in your image. You sent Jesus to earth as a man and used him as an example of the kind of character and life you desire. In its most basic forms, Jesus experienced what I do, yet he sustained his faith and persevered in hardship. You know what I need, oh Lord, because of your wisdom and compassion, and you have provided for your people a great high priest who speaks with authority and compassion regarding my experience and the temptations of life.

I do not understand how he was able to endure so well, or how he was able to withstand temptation so completely, but I know that he has compassion on me. May your precious Holy Spirit help me, mold me, shape me, and guide me along the path to the day of reward, and may I be found worthy of the salvation you have promised in that day.

**How do you think Jesus was perfected in the sufferings he endured?**

# WHOLE AGAIN

The LORD is close to the brokenhearted;
he rescues those whose spirits are crushed.
PSALM 34:17 NLT

Lord, you look after your righteous ones, standing with those who put their hope and trust in you. Though they are attacked, you will rescue them and set them at your right hand. I put my hope in your great promises and seek your will in the earth. Stand with me and be my wingman, and I will be restored. You repair what has been broken. Your heart dwells with those who are distraught and those who have been victims of the world.

I long for the day when I will look upon your face with joy. Bring relief to the brokenhearted and bind up the wounds of those who have suffered. Restore your great creation. Hallelujah!

**How has the Lord helped you deal with brokenness in your life?**

# EMPATHY

Rejoice with those who rejoice, weep with those who weep.
ROMANS 12:15 NRSV

Create in me a heart of love, Father, and help me to live in harmony with all those who are called by your name. You have declared your plans to restore the world after you have exhausted your patience and allowed as many as will come to do so. May my heart follow in the footsteps of your compassion and do good to even those who do not love you. May they see your offering of peace in the way I interact with them and show care.

May your people be blessed in the way I serve them according to your heart. May I have joy in the delight of others and share in the weeping of the brokenhearted. May your will be done in all the earth that we would see the wicked restored rather than destroyed. Thank you for giving freely of your great Spirit and molding my character.

**How do you testify to God's good news of restoration through your empathy with others?**

# As It Should Be

If we know he hears us every time we ask him,
we know we have what we ask from him.
1 JOHN 5:15 NCV

Father, you are good in your ways and wise in regard to the
ways of the world and the good things you desire to see
done. Align my will with your own so I desire to see your
plans accomplished, for I know that you will accomplish all
you have set your heart to do. May I be one who stands in
the gap with you, as Moses did, to plead for you to do the
things you have set to do.

You hear the requests of a righteous man and you will
not fail to bring those requests to pass, for they are in line
with the very things you have desired to do. How joyful
you must be when a man stands with you to see your will
accomplished. May my heart be fully turned your way as I
plead for your will to be done on the earth.

**How do you know that God hears your requests?**

# LIVING ON CAMERA

Whoever walks in integrity walks securely,
but he who makes his ways crooked will be found out.
PROVERBS 10:9 ESV

Father search my deepest desires and motivations and purify me. Change my heart and cause me to seek after you, straightening my path according to your wisdom and good commands. You know me intimately and cannot be tricked. You know my heart better than I do. Reveal the truth to me so I may turn and be cleansed. You have shown me the way to live in righteousness; now help me to do it.

Produce fruit within me according to your good Spirit. May my eyes remain fixed on your righteous promises so I walk directly down the right path. When I look sideways at the distractions of what the world offers, that is when my path goes wrong. You know when I seek after those things because you know my heart. Do not forsake me, Lord, but guide me back to the righteous path.

**How do you think a man can make his way crooked?**

# GLORIFIED

I know that I have not yet reached that goal,
but there is one thing I always do. Forgetting the past
and straining toward what is ahead.

PHILIPPIANS 3:13 NCV

Diligently lead me to the day of your coming, Lord, and give me the strength and persistence to aim toward it with all my being. I turn from the things of my past, the things the world has corrupted and offered in a destructive way, and I look to your Spirit to give me righteous desires that only you can fill.

I look forward to your promise of exaltation and glory to be given to those who straighten their way before you, who persist in doing right, and whose desires are like your own. Magnify this path before me and carry me along by the wisdom of your teaching and the guidance of your Spirit. I long for your promised restoration you have set as our great reward. Be glorified, holy King!

**How do you think traveling the path of righteousness in this life prepares you for life in eternity?**

# FATHER OF GOODNESS

Praise the LORD in song, for He has done excellent things;
Let this be known throughout the earth.
ISAIAH 12:5 NASB

You are worthy of praise and glory, oh God my King, for your works are amazing and the wonder of your powerful ways are beyond compare. You are the author of life, creating the world we see around us. You have established it in beauty and your wisdom and imagination are on full display.

You have established humanity as your governor and image bearer in the earth and devised a marvelous plan to redeem us from our corrupt ways. You have used the works of your enemies to mold and form your own people into the image you have desired, and you have thwarted their attempts to overthrow your rule. You are majestic and magnificent, Almighty God, worthy of all glory and praise.

**Why do the Scriptures insist on God's people remembering his works?**

# LIFE GETS BUSY

The Lord answered her, "Martha, my beloved Martha. Why are you upset and troubled, pulled away by all these many distractions? Are they really that important? Mary has discovered the one thing most important by choosing to sit at my feet. She is undistracted, and I won't take this privilege from her."

LUKE 10:41–42 TPT

Father, the things of life fill my waking thoughts, but I want to focus on the promises you have established. Help me to minimize the importance of things in this life that are so fleeting and give me a renewed excitement for what you plan to do. Energize my devotions with your presence and by your Word.

Fill me with awe and wonder regarding your power and might, giving me little hints of your works in this life so I will not be derailed from the path. Lord, I do live in this age and in these days, but I need your help to accurately prioritize the things that need to be accomplished and reconnect with the things that will hold value for eternity.

**What are some things in your life that seem particularly pressing day-to-day, but won't ultimately be so important? How might these things be recalibrated in your life?**

# With You

We can confidently say,
"The LORD is my helper;
I will not fear;
what can man do to me?"

HEBREWS 13:6 ESV

Lord, fill me with love for your Word and devotion to your promises. May I be humble before you and seek your will rather than my own. Help me to turn from wickedness and embrace your righteousness, trusting in your marvelous good promises. Then, what do I need to fear? No matter what might happen to me, you have promised eternity with you.

Though my body endure hunger, pain, disease, or persecution, still I will stand strong in faith knowing that my redeemer lives, and I shall live again with him forever. Your faithfulness is my support, and I will put my hope in you, the great King of all the earth.

**Can you think of anything you do, or don't do, that derives from a concern for how another person will react to you?**

# In the Fight

The godly may trip seven times, but they will get up again.
But one disaster is enough to overthrow the wicked.
PROVERBS 24:16 NLT

Father, sustain me by your magnificent Word. You know my frailties and the ruggedness of the path of righteousness. My heart is full of many desires that seem easy to fulfill, and the hope of your promises sometimes seems so far away, so I falter. My desire is to follow your ways. Help me to get back up and turn to your truth. It will always be my guidepost to lead me because my heart desires to follow you.

Lord, be gracious to those who do not yet know you and give them the opportunity to respond to your good news. You do not rejoice in the destruction of the wicked but desire to see them repent so they may be saved. Thank you so much for your gracious mercies.

**What does it mean to be wicked? What does it mean to be godly? Why can the godly continue on even after a fall?**

# ABSENT OF JUDGMENT

"Do not judge, and you will not be judged; do not condemn, and you will not be condemned. Forgive, and you will be forgiven."
LUKE 6:37 NRSV

I ask that you give me the wisdom to truly see people, Lord, and approach them out of a position of compassion, as you did, rather than making snap judgments about who they are and what their end will be. Help me to have the grace for them that you have given me, and to treat them with care.

It is against you, and you only, that people sin, so let me not treat them as my own enemies but leave room for you to determine their end. Instead, I wish to call people to turn from their ways while engaging with them as you did. Give me your quality of character and be glorified in the testimony of my actions. Be magnified, oh Lord, in the earth, and let your name be exalted.

**How do you stand firm for righteousness and not be condemning of those who don't walk in righteousness?**

# HONORED

If anyone does not provide for his own,
and especially for those of his household,
he has denied the faith and is worse than an unbeliever.
1 TIMOTHY 5:8 NASB

My Lord, grant me the means and resources to care for those who are in need. May I be your conduit to care for them and protect them. Help me to be faithful and testify to and with them about faith in you.

I give you honor for how you have preserved them and brought them to this day, for it is a blessing to be allowed long life in the world. Give all of us the grace we need to follow your lead, to care for each other, and to love each other as we eagerly await your glorious coming to the earth.

**How can you show honor to a loved one today?**

# STRIVING

"My presence will go with you, and I will give you rest."
EXODUS 33:14 ESV

Oh Lord my God, I am filled with wonder at the way you have worked in the world. For generations, you have been orchestrating world history to lead all nations to one final day of reckoning. Yet through it all, you have exalted your people and have walked with them through the fires and trials of life, to watch over them and to make certain they are preserved to the day of restoration.

Walk with me and strengthen me in the struggle of life. Give me the encouragement and support I need to reach the finish line of this race, and I will look forward to the rest you will provide. May I remain faithful to you, and to your righteousness throughout the process, and I will rejoice in your reward.

**What rest does God have in store for those who strive for him?**

# LESSER THINGS

Let what you heard from the beginning abide in you.
If what you heard from the beginning abides in you,
then you will abide in the Son and in the Father.
1 JOHN 2:24 NRSV

Father, I praise you for your wondrous mercy! You have extended your hand to me, and I am humbled that you have considered me. Give me the strength and wisdom to remain in your wise counsel and to remember the things you have established according to your divine plan. May I continue to hold tightly to the great promises you have made.

I acknowledge your great wisdom in establishing a people for your own possession from among the nations and take hope in the day you restore all things. Be glorified in all things!

**Where can you find the things from the "beginning"?**

# BETTER THAN WINNING

When you do things, do not let selfishness or
pride be your guide. Instead, be humble and
give more honor to others than to yourselves.
PHILIPPIANS 2:3 NCV

My Lord, I look to you to satisfy my need for justice and for righteousness. I know that you have my back and because of this, I can love anyone who mistreats me and I can humbly act when confronted with what I think is injustice. Help me to defer to your wisdom and treat others, especially those whom I think are intentionally treating me poorly, with a positive attitude.

Help me to look for the positive possibilities in their actions, while I allow you to deal with their hearts. Unlike me, you don't judge by mere appearances but, instead, make right judgments. Help me to follow in your steps and put aside my own pride so I see things more clearly.

**How can the Holy Spirit help you to treat someone more humbly?**

# INCREASE MY FAITH

The apostles said to the Lord, "Increase our faith."
LUKE 17:5 NLT

Father, do you know how difficult it often is to put my trust in the truth of your promises? I know that you are God and you rule over all of creation, yet in this age you have granted wicked men to rule over the nations, death to be a rule of life, and difficulty to characterize our daily experience. These are the things that I am bombarded with so often, and it becomes difficult to remember your mighty works of old.

Continually remind me by your Word and your mighty deeds that you are the God who will bring about restoration of the earth, resurrection of my body, and righteous governance of the nations. Help me to believe more fully and more powerfully day-by-day. Thank you that you have poured out your wonderful Holy Spirit to counsel me in these times of difficulty.

**What do you think the purpose of increased faith is?**

# Unmerited Favor

Remember this: sin will not conquer you, for God already has!
You are not governed by law but governed by
the reign of the grace of God.
ROMANS 6:14 TPT

God, you continually amaze me with the way you have
called me and given me an opportunity to be your child. You
called me out of my worldly ways to follow you and seek
your kingdom. You have freed me from the antagonism of
the judgment of your law; I am utterly grateful to you.

Your goodness is beyond my imagination, for I and my
ancestors have been so opposed to you and your ways. I
love that you have not reveled in the destruction of your
enemies but have called out to all nations to turn to you. I
will not be put to shame as I continue to trust in you.

**How has God's unmerited favor blessed you?**

# You Stay

All my longings lie open before you, Lord;
my sighing is not hidden from you.
PSALM 38:9 NIV

I am grateful that you have granted me the right to petition you for forgiveness, Lord. You are willing to hear my pleas for help. You know my desire is to be forgiven and not to continue in sin before you. Give me strength according to your powerful Holy Spirit.

I pray for your restoration and the perseverance to stand strong until the day of your promised return. Do not let my foot slip but sustain me according to your knowledge of my desire to follow you. I place my hope in your righteousness and faithful Word and I trust in your great works. I lay myself before you and, upon your great mercy, I entrust myself to the wisdom of your commands.

**What are the deep longings of your heart?**

# Lessen My Grip

Do not forget to do good and to share,
for with such sacrifices God is well pleased.
HEBREWS 13:16 NKJV

God, I love your Word and your faithfulness to preserve it and fulfill it. I know you have a great plan for my life. Too often my heart has been drawn away from you in order to seek my own preservation, but your good news assures me that even if I go without and I suffer in this life, you will lift me up in the age to come.

I trust in your faithfulness so I will assist my neighbors in their need. I pray, Lord, that you will provide generously to me, not so I may find luxury, but so I may share it with others. Glorify your name, my Lord, in your good gifts. I long to see your name exalted on the lips of the nations.

**What tends to lead you to hold on too tightly to the things you have?**

# UNCONDITIONAL ACCEPTANCE

"All that the Father gives Me will come to Me, and the one who comes to Me I will certainly not cast out."

JOHN 6:37 NASB

May my desires be turned fully to you, oh Lord my God, and may your name be glorified in my life. Prepare me so that I am found worthy to attend your great celebration. Your name is worthy to be exalted, and you have freely extended your hand of fellowship to me; grant me the wisdom to know how to treat that gift with the honor it deserves.

Clear me of my transgressions against you and grant me permission to approach your glorious throne with confidence in the righteousness of your ways. You are faithful in all your ways, and you will not hold faultless those who treat your goodness lightly or with contempt. Your goodness is humbling and sobering; may it return to you a great reward. Be glorified, oh great God!

**What does coming to Jesus entail?**

# AIM FOR HARMONY

Let us aim for harmony in the church
and try to build each other up.
ROMANS 14:19 NLT

Father, you know how different we all are, for you have
knitted us together and have loved our diversity. Give us a
united heart for your good news and singular hope for your
restoration so that we may all work together for the same
goal. Help us to live in unity and harmony with each other
rather than seeking after our individual goals and
personal agendas.

Help me to seek to encourage my fellow believer in
the good and righteous hope that you have set before
us according to your good news. Help me to put aside
temporary satisfaction in favor of uplifting fellowship based
on your promises. Help us to remain unified around your
good news and keep us from splintering into various
factions based on things outside of your will.

**What is the goal of harmony in the congregation
of God?**

# June

"Whatever you ask in prayer, believe that you have received it, and it will be yours."

MARK 11:24 ESV

# DEPENDABLE

Let not steadfast love and faithfulness forsake you;
bind them around your neck;
write them on the tablet of your heart.
PROVERBS 3:3 ESV

Glorious King, you are faithful and true in all your ways. You do not turn back on your promises but fulfill them in their appropriate time. Your yes means yes, and your no means no. I have no reason to doubt the truth of your goodness. Develop in me the same trustworthiness. Make this an integral part of my character.

I want to be someone whom others can depend on because I have bound your love and faithfulness around my neck. Help me to show your goodness to those around me. I rely on you for everything, God, and I know you will not disappoint me.

**What does dependability in your words and actions signify regarding your faith?**

# I WILL REJOICE

This is the day the LORD has made;
We will rejoice and be glad in it.
PSALM 118:24 NKJV

Oh Lord, King of the heavens and the earth, I exalt you for the day you have set forth. Every day reminds us that you are faithful. You have said that as long as the days proceed forward into history, you will also remain faithful to your promises. Each day reminds me of your goodness and I am so grateful to you for that.

I am filled with joy and excitement each day as I look forward to spending eternity with you. Thank you for daily reminders of your mercy and grace that help me continue striving toward the finish line. I exalt you, my King, and praise your wonderful name, for you are good in all your magnificent ways.

**What makes this day joyful for you?**

# With All

The man answered, "Love the LORD your God with all your heart, all your soul, all your strength, and all your mind." Also, "Love your neighbor as you love yourself."

LUKE 10:27 NCV

With everything in me I want to be devoted to your ways, God, for you are incomparable in your power, majesty, and wisdom. Often, I have sought after men with worldly wisdom, seeking wealth or adventure, vengeance or security, yet none of them could deliver true satisfaction as you are able to do.

You have shown yourself to be the God who deserves all praise and glory. Help me to devote myself to honoring you in word and deed, loving others in honesty and truth so they might turn from their antagonism toward you and find fulfillment. I choose to withhold satisfying my ungodly desires in devotion to your good gifts. You are the only one who ought to have my full dedication. Thank you for accepting me into your family.

**How do you devote yourself fully to God?**

# EVERY MOMENT

Teach us to number our days,
that we may gain a heart of wisdom.
PSALM 90:12 NIV

Oh Lord, you are the source of life. You watch my steps and guide my paths. Help me to remember the shortness of life, how the years I experience are but a moment in the grand scheme of things. Then I might realize that living for my full satisfaction in this time frame is not worth the effort I put into it.

You live forever and have promised us life everlasting as we put our faith and trust in you. Fill me with wisdom to remember the promises you have made. My work is much more valuable when I devote it to attaining eternal satisfaction, when the years of enjoyment will continue into forever.

**What wisdom comes from recognizing the length of your life?**

# ALL GRACE

After you suffer for a short time, God, who gives all grace, will
make everything right. He will make you strong and support you
and keep you from falling. He called you to share in his glory in
Christ, a glory that will continue forever.

1 PETER 5:10 NCV

Strengthen me, Father, as you strengthened Jesus in the
garden before his death, to endure the suffering that comes
to those who choose to align themselves with you in this
life. Encourage me to stand firm in the face of trials and
difficulties. I know that I will not suffer forever.

Remind me of your goodness and favor and help me to offer
a true testimony of your good news so others are drawn to
give you their lives. I can endure all things for your name
because of your faithfulness and the wonder of your
great promises.

**How do you see God's grace in your ability to endure
difficulties?**

# Humble Help

If another believer is overcome by some sin, you who are godly
should gently and humbly help that person back onto the right
path. And be careful not to fall into the same temptation yourself.

GALATIANS 6:1 NLT

Father, help me to be a kind brother to your people, so I
am one who encourages and helps to restore those who
have fallen. Jesus was strong in his words, but to those
who sought him, he would gently guide them. I know that
you have no tolerance for sin, so give me the wisdom I
need to know how to be gentle and humble without being
permissive.

Help me to be merciful and not overly condemning of those
who need to be rebuked. I know that I am not my brother's
savior, so I humbly offer my services to you to serve my
brothers and sisters righteously. Thank you for your great
mercy to me.

**Have you ever experienced a time when you felt
condemned for sin in your life rather than assisted in
overcoming it?**

# BEFORE CONFESSING

If we confess our sins, he who is faithful and just will forgive us our sins and cleanse us from all unrighteousness.

1 JOHN 1:9 NRSV

My Lord and God, I ask for your mercy for me in my weaknesses. I own my faults before you and will not attempt to shift responsibility for my actions. I have missed the target you have set and at times have not even been aiming to hit the appropriate goal. I have no one to blame but myself and I confess to you my wrongdoing, humbly taking responsibility for my actions.

I am not a victim of circumstance or subject to someone else's suggestion, but I made a decision and I own the wrong I have done. Forgive me, compassionate Judge, for my actions before you and how I have rebelled against your righteous rule. I turn to you and pledge my devotion to you again. Cleanse me according to your mercy and teach me the way leading to life everlasting. I am not worthy to receive any good gift from you, but I am grateful to you for your offer of peace.

**What do you need to confess to the Lord today? Do you know that he offers forgiveness and mercy when you ask for it?**

# WE ARE FAMILY

I bow my knees before the Father, from whom every family in
heaven and on earth is named.
EPHESIANS 3:14–15 ESV

Lord, I belong to you and you have authority over me. I
submit myself to you. Your right of authority makes me
part of your family. You have accepted the responsibility
to provide for my needs and to care for me in my times of
distress and difficulty.

I thank you for the way you have compassionately invited
me into your family and embraced me as a beloved son.
Though I have given you no reason to accept me, you
have reached out your hand of peace. I am humbled that
you have accepted me and you are treating me like a son,
guiding and disciplining me to follow your righteous path. I
am yours, mighty God; my devotion belongs to you.

**What effect does being part of God's family have on
your perspective?**

# My Deepest Pain

"Blessed are those who mourn, for they shall be comforted."
MATTHEW 5:4 NASB

You see my inmost heart, God; you know my deepest
wounds and fears. You have seen into my depths and you
know the source of my actions. You are the God of healing,
and you bind up the wounds if I come to you and confess
my need. You are kind to the humble. You love the contrite,
and you restore the heart of those who mourn. You know
the heartache caused by sickness and death in the world,
and you are intent on eradicating it, but for a time, you allow
it to bring us to our knees and find our hope in you.

Bind up my wounds and let them strengthen my heart and
my compassion for others. Do not let it harden me against
my neighbor. Help me to feel the pain and let it work itself
into righteousness. My instinct is to flee from such intense
pain, but if I will trust you and stand fast. You are faithful to
work with it unto the fulfillment of a kingdom where we will
all receive comfort beyond compare.

**Can you identify places where pain has hardened you?
How can that be reversed?**

# Pay It Forward

Remember that judgment is merciless for the one
who judges others without mercy. So by showing mercy
you take dominion over judgment!
JAMES 2:13 TPT

Father, I am overjoyed at the mercy you have shown me
because I have much cause to fear your judgment. Thank
you for offering me peace in place of destruction and giving
me confidence in your glorious promises. You are working
in me to develop a godly attitude and a compassionate
heart. Help my heart to never forget the kindness you have
shown me so I will act with mercy toward others who also
need your mercy. I know that if I repay other people harshly
when I have been offered such peace, I will not receive the
promise you will reveal.

I am moved by your compassion for me; strengthen me
to act likewise. May those who deserve your wrath and
judgment come to know your abundant mercy and choose
to take your offer of peace. Then I will celebrate in the
salvation of many brothers and. Help my compassionate
attitude to mirror your own so you will be more greatly
exalted.

**Do you find it difficult at times to offer mercy to
some people?**

# SECURITY

"Behold, I will bring to it health and healing,
and I will heal them and reveal to them
abundance of prosperity and security."
JEREMIAH 33:6 ESV

Father, you have given abundantly the tools I need to
endure in this life, and your promises are certain to restore
and bless abundantly in the resurrection. I will gain refuge in
the certainty of your promises so I can boldly face trouble.
The promise of your restoration is a source of strength that
guides me and because of it I can walk confidently even in
uncertain times.

Help me to trust in your sovereign power which the enemy
cannot thwart. Though your enemies rage against you and
your people in this life, though they bring destruction and
death, I have confidence that you will restore what the
enemy has destroyed and you will heal the wounds that
have been inflicted. Magnify your great name in all the earth.

**If we will endure troubles in this life, where can
security be found?**

# For Your Glory

"Seek first His kingdom and His righteousness,
and all these things will be added to you."
Matthew 6:33 nasb

Lord, many are the concerns and anxious circumstances of life in this world. So often I catch myself concerned about what job I will have or how to pay for the next bill, but the goal that truly matters is the establishing of your kingdom. From that point, all my needs will be provided in abundance, and I will lack no good thing.

No longer will anyone be anxious about the next day or what it may hold, but your support will uphold us in peace and safety. Your right hand will sustain us, and you will strengthen us to accomplish the tasks you set before us, and we will have no need to be afraid that our lives will be in danger from lack of provision. Help me to daily set my goal squarely on the life that is to come and put all my hope in you.

**Have you had times when you wondered why the Lord seemed very slow in providing?**

# Reason for Success

The LORD will be your confidence,
And will keep your foot from being caught.
PROVERBS 3:26 NASB

I would have you fill me with wisdom and understanding of your design, oh Lord, that with the power of your Spirit you might deliver me safely to the day of your blessed renewal. Your kingdom is full of delight and joy, provision is prevalent, and the wealth of beauty is beyond compare. You have dreamed of the glory of your creation for ages, and soon you will bring it to glorious fruition.

May your wisdom give me the ability to attain all you have promised and fill me with confidence of your works. I put my trust in you as you strengthen me to succeed in achieving the goal of my faith. Be honored for your merciful works in my life, dear God.

**Why is the Lord your confidence?**

# My Parachute

When I am afraid,
I will put my trust in you.
PSALM 56:3 NLT

According to the power and desire of your Holy Spirit, refresh the basis of my trust in you, God. My life is short, and death comes to all of us in this age, yet you will restore what has been taken and you will give life back to the righteous. When I begin to turn again to the fear of the world and fear of suffering or losing my life, may your Spirit encourage me with the knowledge of your coming glory. Then I will prepare myself to endure the trial before you, in your name, and give my life as a testimony of your love and mercy.

I will trust in you because you are worthy to be trusted, you who have fulfilled your promises in the past and continue to reach your hand of peace out to Jew and Gentile alike, just as you have declared you would. Give me courage to face the world through my fear and to overcome it as you did.

**What gives you the ability to face the difficulties of life?**

# Bloom

Grow in the grace and knowledge of our Lord and Savior Jesus
Christ. To him be glory both now and forever! Amen.
2 Peter 3:18 NIV

Oh Lord, I ask you to build me up in your character, molding
me according to your image. Transform my desires to look
more like yours, day-by-day, and conform my thoughts to
focus on the day of your return. Renew hope in me through
the knowledge and understanding I gain in the instruction of
your Word.

Teach me the paths you have set forth me. Help me to
proclaim your name in the earth and spread the knowledge
of your good news to those around me that they may
joyfully exalt you. I am overwhelmed with your magnificence,
and I glorify you for your perfect wisdom.

**What stands out to you most vibrantly about Jesus?**

# THOUGHTS CAPTURED

Think about the things that are good and worthy of praise.
Think about the things that are true and honorable
and right and pure and beautiful and respected.
PHILIPPIANS 4:8 NCV

God, take hold of my mind and reveal to me your magnificence. This Scripture speaks of the things upon which I desire to focus. Grow my understanding and appreciation for them so that the fearful things of this life fade in comparison. Let even the selfish joys of this life lose their luster. I long to rejoice in you—and with you—over the works you will perform in my life and in the lives of others.

Restore to me each day the joy of such things. According to your will and in the power of your Spirit, daily draw my attention to the works you are highlighting, the ones you want people to see so they may be encouraged to wait on you. In my times of distress, may my thoughts turn to you, and I will be glad.

**How can you change the kinds of things you desire to set your mind on?**

# CHOOSE YOUR WAY

A man without self-control
is like a city broken into and left without walls.
PROVERBS 25:28 ESV

I am amazed to learn that self-control is considered a fruit of the Holy Spirit. It sounds ironic that an effect of the Spirit's work in my life is self-control, yet you are molding my character and forming me into your image, Jesus, the image you originally had in mind when you created humanity. Build in me the ability to control my impulses, to act according to my own will and not in reaction to whatever may occur.

Teach me to own my character, desires, and impulses rather than treating myself as a victim of these things. Then I will be able to use them in service to your plans and will, to your glory and exaltation. You have not sought to establish humanity on the earth to be victimized by our whims or paralyzed by fear of what we may do, but you desire men who exhibit control over themselves and can glorify you in their work. Be glorified, Lord!

**Why is a lack of self-control such a devastating characteristic?**

# Good Sense

Those with good sense are slow to anger,
and it is their glory to overlook an offense.
PROVERBS 19:11 NRSV

Father, I ask you—who are a giver of good gifts—to fill me
with your wisdom in order to act rightly toward other people.
Help me to truly and deeply grasp the certainty of your
promised restoration and of the things you will accomplish
so I may make right choices in my daily life.

I know that you will bring justice with you in the day of
accounting, so I do not need to be concerned that I am
being mistreated without recourse. Help me to overlook the
actions of those who misuse me in order that I might show
them the greatness of your mercy through my sharing with
them the reason for my forbearance.

**What are some of the reasons you ought to overlook
the ways people may mistreat you? Why is this
considered good?**

# CONTENTMENT

Each of you should continue to live in whatever situation
the Lord has placed you, and remain as you were
when God first called you.

1 CORINTHIANS 7:17 NLT

Father, I put my hope in your promises and not in the things I can see and attain in this life. I am content with what you have promised, and I put aside the desire to better my position for my own sake. I will give you my hopes and desires and trust you will provide for my needs and be good to me. I will leave my situation in your hands and allow you to change my circumstances according to your will, and not with my own strength or ambition.

I defer to you as my King and leader for your wisdom is exceptional and will guide me to the day when I may receive the prize of salvation you have in store. I exalt you, God, and I step back so you may be glorified. May your will and commands be fulfilled in the earth.

**Why are you called to be content with your
life situation?**

# ULTIMATE GUIDE

I want you to pattern your lives after me,
just as I pattern mine after Christ.
1 CORINTHIANS 11:1 TPT

Merciful Father, how I thank you for the examples of godly living you have placed in the world. While you have given me your Word and not left me without instruction, you have also placed people around me to show me what your character looks like. Help me to follow their example and become an example to others so that we all may be like Jesus in love, compassion, strength, righteousness, and obedience.

I thank you that you have graciously raised up men after your own heart among the nations who are able to guide others to the truth of your good news. Magnify your name in them so that they may glorify you.

**What does Paul mean when he says, "For your sake, I fill up in my body what is lacking in the sufferings of Christ"?**

# NOTHING TO CONDEMN

There is now no condemnation for
those who are in Christ Jesus.
ROMANS 8:1 NASB

Draw me ever closer to you, God, and make me more like
Jesus. Thank you for making a way for me to be forgiven
of the wrongs I have committed against you and showing
me the example in Jesus' character of the kind of man you
value and reward. I accept yet again the offer of peace you
have extended to me based on Jesus' sacrificial death and
seek to honor his sacrifice by living as he did.

You testified to the fact that Jesus was the type of man you
value, the kind of man you exalt and reward, by resurrecting
him from crucifixion death. You have appointed him to sit on
the throne and you will reward those who see his example
and follow it with everlasting life in his righteous kingdom.
Grant me forgiveness, Lord, according to your Word and will,
and I will rejoice in you.

**Why do you not have to fear condemnation?**

# Never Too Big

> "You don't have enough faith," Jesus told them. "I tell you the truth, if you had faith even as small as a mustard seed, you could say to this mountain, 'Move from here to there,' and it would move. Nothing would be impossible."
>
> MATTHEW 17:20 NLT

What is your desire, Lord? What do you intend to do? Teach me your ways and the path you have established. Show me the end before it comes so I may trust in you to fulfill your goal. Then, I will stand in the power of your Spirit and accomplish the task you set before me. I will successfully achieve the goal you have set because I have believed you.

You desire to establish your people in righteousness and to bless the nations of the earth through them. You will renew the earth for the sake of your image bearers. I trust in your loving faithfulness to your promised decrees and I will succeed in attaining the end of this path because I believe you. No matter what obstacle I face, it will not be able to thwart me in winning the prize.

**How is your level of faith today?**

# SELFLESSNESS

Let each of you look out not only for his own interests,
but also for the interests of others.
PHILIPPIANS 2:4 NKJV

Lord, I love your heart of compassion for others. You extend
a hand of friendship even to your enemies in the hopes
that they will turn and give you their allegiance. Though
they pervert their ways and seek to corrupt the earth,
abusing and misusing the good things you have created,
you seek their salvation and desire to give them good
gifts. May my heart likewise be filled with such a caring and
compassionate tendency to look out for the interests of
others, despite their attitude toward me.

Father, as one who bears your image, I desire justice,
and injustice infuriates me. I long to see your righteous
rule become the norm in the earth; even so, teach me to
patiently endure hardship and trials for the sake of the
wicked—for a time—until your righteous timing is fulfilled.
According to your Holy Spirit, I am willing to wait to see my
benefit until more people turn to you.

**What is the hardest part of selfless living for you?**

# MAKE YOU PROUD

Do your best to present yourself to God as one approved by him,
a worker who has no need to be ashamed,
rightly explaining the word of truth.

2 TIMOTHY 2:15 NRSV

Father, you have given me a gift I could never repay in the
promise of salvation and everlasting life. Though I have
been your enemy, still you have offered me peace. Now,
I ask you to build in me a character and a spirit worthy to
receive the gift you are offering so that I will not put you
to shame.

Fill me with your Spirit of wisdom and understanding and
give me strength in your Spirit to persevere in the training
process, not abandoning it in the middle. I want you to be
glorified and your attendants to have been made ready to
receive you when you come. Prepare me to receive the
hope of my faith, and may my presence be pleasing to you
in that day.

**How can you present yourself to God as approved
by him?**

# TAKE COURAGE

"Have I not commanded you? Be strong and of good courage;
do not be afraid, nor be dismayed, for the LORD your God
is with you wherever you go."
JOSHUA 1:9 NKJV

Father, I know the plans you have for me; I know the
promises you have made to bring blessing to all the earth;
I know that you have determined to restore all things
and bring goodness and righteousness back. You will go
before me and deliver me from those who wish to see me
destroyed, and you will raise me up and establish me in
your righteousness.

I trust that you are one who fulfills your Word. Lord, give
me courage and strength to endure in those times when
you seem so far from me. Help me to remember your good
promises and your trustworthiness. Even when things seem
dark and difficult, the light of your Word will shine forth to
give me hope. I glorify you for your greatness and righteous
love and faithfulness.

**Have you ever had a difficult time being encouraged
that God is with you during difficult times? Why does it
sometimes seem so difficult to hold on to the promise
of God's presence?**

# Forgive Me

Consider my affliction and my trouble,
and forgive all my sins.
Psalm 25:18 esv

Precious Lord, be merciful to me and give me peace. Help me in my troubles and give me rest from my difficulties. I trust in you for deliverance, and I ask you for your forgiveness of my disobedience to your commands. Lord, I turn to you and give you my heart. Please accept my devotion now despite how I lived in opposition to you.

I put my hope in your deliverance and salvation, trusting in your great promises and choosing to be satisfied with the good things you offer to those who humble themselves before you. Though I deserve your judgment and retribution, I ask you to remember me when you come to establish righteousness in the earth and raise me up with your people. I exalt your name and desire your righteous rulership. Thank you for considering my request.

**Do you need to ask for forgiveness today?**

# New Heart

"He who believes in Me, as the Scripture has said,
out of his heart will flow rivers of living water."
JOHN 7:38 NKJV

Father, I turn to you and seek your goodness. I am grateful to you for your great mercy and the way you have provided a way of salvation. You will restore the earth in your might and glory and will establish righteousness, exalting the righteous and giving everlasting life to all who put their hope and trust in you.

In your great wisdom, train me to act with compassion and mercy toward all. Fill me with the wisdom and understanding that will result in increased faith so my attitudes and actions will reflect your goodness. I pray that many will see and hear the message of life as it flows from you through me and inspires many to turn to you. By your grace, I will be a blessing to others and serve well. May my heart be devoted to loving you and loving others so all are blessed in your name.

**What differentiates believers from non-believers who seem to care for others?**

# By Your Grace

"If you forgive those who sin against you,
your heavenly Father will forgive you. But if you refuse to
forgive others, your Father will not forgive your sins."
MATTHEW 6:14–15 NLT

Lord my God, you have been incomparably merciful to me in your forgiveness and the peace offering you extended to me. You have given me the opportunity to join with your people and will not hold my wicked acts against me. Though my actions have often led to the hurting of others, still you have granted me pardon because I have believed in you. Thank you for your great compassion.

How can I hold anything against my neighbor? What offense could I have experienced that makes a grudge worthwhile? I will give my cause over to you, God, and I will give my neighbor compassion as you have shown me. I put my trust in you and offer peace to my enemy and to any who might despitefully use me. You have done great things for me and I desire to do all I can to share that testimony with others. I hope you will be pleased with my offering of praise.

**What are some offenses, against yourself or against others, that you have felt justified in not forgiving?**

# How Much

"The very hairs of your head are all numbered."
MATTHEW 10:30 NKJV

How much have you cared for me, God, and sought to do good to me? I can hardly consider the depths of the actions you have taken to offer redemption to me, though I certainly have not been worthy to deserve it. You have been faithful to your promises that all who once rejected you might know your offer of peace and your promise of glorious restoration.

Though I had been opposed to your governance, you sustained me and provided for my needs. You have placed me in a world of great beauty which produces food, water, and air for my daily needs. You have watched over me and protected me in many instances when I was in danger, even when I did not know it. The ways you have seen fit to look out for me are manifold, and I will give you my devotion. I trust in you regardless of the challenges I face, and I look forward to facing them in your name. Be glorified, my Lord.

**What are some specific ways God has shown you how much he cares?**

# All Authority

"All authority in heaven and on earth has been given to me."
MATTHEW 28:18 NIV

My Lord, you are a good and righteous King, and your rule is better than all the kings of the nations. I long for the day that your authority is established. I trust your faithfulness to establish what you have set forth to do. I am so excited to see your righteous rule go forward in all the world and see my own nation's leaders submitting to your righteous decrees.

How good and pleasant it will be when you restore the whole earth by your righteous acts! I trust that even now what occurs in the earth will work out for the benefit of all who call upon your name in faith. How marvelous it is to know that you are working all things out according to your plan of redemption for the earth.

**What authority do you have in Jesus' name?**

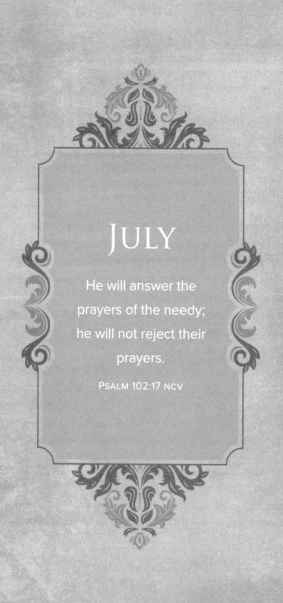

# July

He will answer the
prayers of the needy;
he will not reject their
prayers.

PSALM 102:17 NCV

# DELETING CRITICISM

Do not let any unwholesome talk come out of your mouths, but
only what is helpful for building others up according to their
needs, that it may benefit those who listen.

EPHESIANS 4:29 NIV

Father help me to be an encourager to others and not
a person who tears them down or discourages them. I
don't want to be the kind of person who causes others
to feel inadequate. Help me to be kind in my words, with
graciousness, even if at times I need to be stern. Let my
words not be the kind that tear down but that build up. May
other believers walk away from me filled with determination
in their continued walk of faith.

Lord, I don't want to be the kind of person who belittles
others to feel better about myself. Keep my eyes trained on
your coming promises so that I will train my tongue to speak
well to people. May you be glorified by my words not only
in worship but in my daily conversations because of the
kindness of the way I speak. Thank you for giving me your
Holy Spirit to guide and direct my heart and my words.

**How can your words be made more wholesome
while still maintaining the ability to have fun with
your friends?**

# Your Reasons

Every man's way is right in his own eyes,
But the LORD weighs the hearts.
PROVERBS 21:2 NASB

Oh God, you don't judge people according to the way they appear to be, but you know what truly motivates them. You judge rightly and you see what is at the heart of people's actions. Mold me and shape me according to your Spirit. Conform my heart and its desires to the character of your Son, whose character you approved because you rewarded him with resurrection from death. This same gift you will give all who exhibit the same desires and actions as Jesus.

I ask that you give me the desire to be like Jesus in his life and in his sacrificial example. Know my heart and my ways, and may they be found acceptable to you. You do not reward the proud, but you are willing to exalt the humble and those who serve you in truth. Be magnified in me and use me as an example to the world of the kind of man you reward.

**Why is it important for your heart to be right before God when your actions seem beneficial?**

# WHILE I WAIT

They desire a better, that is, a heavenly country.
Therefore God is not ashamed to be called their God,
for He has prepared a city for them.
HEBREWS 11:16 NKJV

Oh Lord my God, I long for the day of your glorious appearing when you bring with you the salvation you have promised—restoration, resurrection, and renewal. I look forward to a beautiful, glorious city from which blessing and provision will spread to all the nations of the earth.

Oh, what a day that will be when you finally put an end to wickedness and replace it with righteousness! What a magnificent party we will have in your honor as you bring to fulfillment your promises. I wait with anticipation for that day and encourage you to bring it in your great wisdom and mercy. Strengthen and encourage me in the meantime to be faithful to you as I wait. Do not be ashamed of me but remember me as your son.

**What are you anticipating from God in the life to come?**

# I AM FREE

"Then you will know the truth, and the truth will make you free."
JOHN 8:32 NCV

Father, the rulers of the nations are confused and have become corrupt in their thinking. Many ask, like Pilate asked of Jesus, "What is truth?" Truth is relatively simple yet more complicated than many can grasp: the ways of the world we are so used to seeing are not the natural way of things. You will judge the world according to your righteousness; you will establish your throne, and justice will flow forth to heal the nations. You will restore the dead and deliver the sick; you will make the desert sprout in abundant growth and streams will flow in dry places, and no one will suffer lack.

Your righteous will and glorious blessing will flow to all who have persevered in waiting patiently for your day; they will taste the good fruit of your kingdom. May you accomplish this soon, Lord, and grant me a portion with you according to your mercy.

**From what are you freed in Jesus?**

# SIMPLICITY

I'm afraid that just as Eve was deceived by the serpent's clever lies, your thoughts may be corrupted and you may lose your single-hearted devotion and pure love for Christ.

2 CORINTHIANS 11:3 TPT

Oh Lord, many interpretations and philosophies can creep into the pure message you desire the world to know and to heed, but I ask that you help clarify it for me and keep my mind set fully on the good news that belongs to you. Reinforce in me the confidence I have in the promises you have made and help me not to mistake or misuse them for false comfort.

You have promised me everlasting life and unbreakable health and wellbeing in the age to come, but in this life, I will face trouble. You have promised me abundant food and drink even in the most desolate places in the age to come, but in this life, I am to learn to be content in hunger and plenty for either could be my circumstance. Let my heart not become fearful of the things I will face in this life, for then I may pervert your good news and seek to establish righteousness according to my own understanding. Keep me in your wise counsel, God.

**How has God helped to correct false interpretations in your life?**

# A Season

For everything there is a season,
and a time for every matter under heaven.
ECCLESIASTES 3:1 NRSV

Lord, I ask you to fill me with the contentment I need to be flexible in any situation I face. You have said that my circumstances may be very fluid, at times enjoying peace and relative prosperity and at times suffering hunger and poverty. Give me what I need so I will not become attached to the good things I enjoy, knowing that the blessings of the next life are far better.

In this life, the seasons turn, and at times wicked rulers follow good ones, and poor circumstances follow good ones. I need the help of your Holy Spirit to know when to standby and when to seek refuge, when to speak out and when to hold my peace. You orchestrate the circumstances of the world to bring about your desired effects. Help me to act appropriately in every season, for you will initiate the season of full restoration.

**How does knowing that each season of life is temporary help you?**

# Not Defeated

Every child of God defeats this evil world,
and we achieve this victory through our faith.
1 JOHN 5:4 NLT

Father, I ask you to increase my faith. I believe you are the God of all creation who created the heavens and the earth and filled them with life. I believe that you made humanity in your image. I believe that you will one day renew the creation and reverse the curse you put on it and put an end to wicked governance. Yet my heart's desires still tend to wander. Strengthen my faith and increase it so that my heart will more fully place its hope in you, and my eyes will stay more focused on the future prize rather than present gratification.

I will devote myself increasingly to train my heart to long for the things you desire rather than being satisfied with this world. You will give me victory because I believe your Word and seek to purify myself according to your desires. Thank you for your promised salvation. Thank you for showing me the path I can take to attain victory. Be glorified in me.

**How can God be glorified in your victories?**

# WILLINGLY TETHERED

Perfume and incense bring joy to the heart,
and the pleasantness of a friend
springs from their heartfelt advice.
PROVERBS 27:9 NIV

Increase your body, Father, and expand your influence in the earth. Grow fellowship between your people and help us to find abundant love and care for each other. Help us to be unified in our pursuit of the same goal. May we adore the brotherhood and closeness that comes of drinking from your Spirit's wisdom and instruction. The joy and contentment which come from sharing this walk together is incomparable.

Like a sports team training together and striving toward the same goal, develop in us camaraderie and sacrificial love. I am glad to call your people "brothers and sisters," and I hope for a great increase of this family before the day of glory. Draw me closer to your family and increase my love and compassion, helping me to support and accept support. Thank you for your great and magnificent provision of fellowship.

**What do you see as your greatest obstacle to deeper fellowship?**

# WHATEVER I ASK

"If in my name you ask me for anything, I will do it."
JOHN 14:14 NRSV

Your ways are righteous, God, and your plans are without equal in their goodness. You have established them from the beginning of creation and will restore them fully.
You desire to bless the nations and establish a holy and righteous humanity in the age to come. I know that you will do these things and I have set my heart on receiving such blessings. I have turned myself away from self-preservation and self-exaltation and instead want you to be glorified.

I am satisfied with merely being accepted into your kingdom. I ask for your will to be done in the earth just as it is in the heavens. I will submit to you and let you determine the course of my path, and I will follow you to the ends of space and time. I am devoted to you, kind Father, so fulfill my requests of you. I can trust that you will fulfill whatever I ask in the name of your anointed Messiah, Jesus, since I have committed to aligning my own desires with yours. Be favorable to my requests and may they bring glory to your name and produce righteousness in my heart.

**Does asking for something in Jesus' name merely mean invoking his name in the prayer?**

# MUCH NEED

Even lions may get weak and hungry,
but those who look to the LORD will have every good thing.
PSALM 34:10 NCV

Heavenly Father, you have established your creation to
provide nourishment and the necessities of life to the
creatures you have put here. Yet, because of humanity's
rebellion against you, you placed a curse on the earth that
sometimes results in famine and lack of provision. These
circumstances afford opportunities for humans to learn
humility and to seek you for redemption. I ask you
to support me and care for me as I place my trust in you.
I know you are faithful to uphold those who rely on you
in humility.

I am insufficient on my own to take care of myself. You are
the one who not only provides the air I breathe but the
material of which I am made. You will establish me for your
name's sake according to your glorious promises. You will
provide abundantly more than I can ask or imagine. Lord, I
need you. I am still weak on my own and all my strength is
not sufficient to save myself. You are my strength and my
shield. I depend on you.

**How do you depend on God to sustain you?**

# BEARING GIFTS

There are varieties of gifts, but the same Spirit. And there are varieties of ministries, and the same Lord. There are varieties of effects, but the same God who works all things in all persons. But to each one is given the manifestation of the Spirit for the common good.

1 CORINTHIANS 12:4–7 NASB

Oh Lord my God, what a marvelous gift you have provided to us for the building up of your Church: your Holy Spirit. The Spirit imparts your desires and teaches me what motivates your work. He encourages and strengthens, supports and teaches, empowers and directs people to trust in you for their every need. Each of your children has a gift to use. Help me to use my gift for you and keep me from falling into the trap of using it for selfish gain or promoting a false understanding of your good news.

You have called us to set our gaze on you and not seek our comfort in this life. Instead, may your Spirit teach me and others to put aside the desire to gain worldly things and to hope in the things that will be revealed from the heavens at Jesus' return. Your gifts are good, and they produce good fruit in my life; sustain me in keeping with your faithful love through the power of these beautiful gifts.

**What are your spiritual gifts? How do you use them to honor the Lord?**

# BELOVED CHILD

You are altogether beautiful, my love;
there is no flaw in you.
SONG OF SOLOMON 4:7 ESV

My Lord, diligently prepare me to receive the reward of
my faith and cleanse me according to your righteous love.
You are faithful to fulfill your promises and among those
is the promise to replace in me the heart of stone I have
developed with a soft heart that is submitted to your good
teachings and reflects your compassionate mercy.

You have shown me the way of faith and righteousness.
Help me to be found ready, awake and fully alert to the
signs of the times, teaching others and helping them to
make themselves ready as well. I love your teaching,
Father, so I ask that it wash over me and cleanse me from
the unrighteousness that can so easily entangle. I pray
you would be glorified through the work you will have
accomplished in and through me.

**How does God make you ready to receive him at
his coming?**

# SADNESS

Cast all your anxiety on him, because he cares for you.
1 PETER 5:7 NRSV

Thank you for looking out for me and supporting me in life, God. You see me, and that humbles me. Who am I that you would consider me, much less care about my life and the path I walk? Yet here I stand before you. I seek your comfort, for life is troublesome and the weight of care and anxiety are heavy upon my mind and heart.

I confess to you that I do not possess enough strength or knowledge to solve my troubles and reconcile my circumstances, so I lay my cares before you. Give me your wisdom so I will be able to face life with confidence in you. I love to hear your words of comfort and encouragement for they help me to feel like I am a part of something bigger than myself. You give me worthwhile purpose and a goal to achieve. Thank you for accepting my offering and not bypassing me in my weakness.

**Do you have confidence to approach God with your weaknesses and the anxieties that can lead you to falter?**

# BEAUTIFUL FUTURE

> "No eye has seen, no ear has heard,
> and no mind has imagined
> what God has prepared
> for those who love him."
>
> 1 CORINTHIANS 2:9 NLT

I cannot imagine the plans you have in store for your children, God, and it thrills my heart to consider the depth of the blessing you will pour out. Your goodness is incomparable, and my experience is so shaded in suffering and pain. How can I possibly conceive of the future you have in store for the righteous who hope in your coming kingdom?

Your benevolent heart is beautiful in its disposition toward me. I am humbled that you would invite me to take part in this gift, for nothing I have done makes me deserving of it, but my heart thrills at the suggestion of your glory. I have devoted myself to you and chosen to love you. May you find great joy in my sacrifice to you.

**Do you ever find it difficult to hope in the future because you've never experienced anything to compare it with?**

# A VOICE

He will care for the needy and neglected
when they cry to him for help.
The humble and helpless will know his kindness,
for with a father's compassion he will save their souls.
PSALM 72:12-13 TPT

Fill me with compassion for other people, Lord, and open my eyes to see beyond my own circle. You care for the oppressed and the needy with diligence and will provide for their needs. I need to be reminded that the humble of spirit are the ones who will receive good gifts from you, but the proud and arrogant will be cast to the ground in shame.

Help me to declare your kindness to those who have been humbled by life and give me the resources to take care of their needs. May their hearts cry to you for sustenance rather than putting their trust in any other provision. May your name be glorified because you, the greatest of Kings, have taken up the cause of those the world considers the least worthy. Help me to be your ambassador to those who need to be encouraged. May your Word bring forth fruit in the hearts of those who have nowhere else to go because you can certainly be trusted to deliver on your promises.

**What advantage do the poor and needy have over others when it comes to the kingdom of God?**

# OBEDIENCE

I will keep on obeying your instructions
forever and ever.
PSALM 119:44 NLT

Father, you know my heritage, that I come from idolatrous people who have rebelled against you, the only great God and creator of all things. Still, you have reached out to me and invited me to join you in your family. I seek to honor your great mercy and I devote myself to your cause, to see your good news spread forth to all nations and to call your people to turn back to you.

Through you, I will encourage the downtrodden with the message of your justice, and I will warn the arrogant with the message of your limited restraint. I will strengthen the brokenhearted with the message of your restoration, and I will comfort the hungry with the message of uninterrupted provision. I trust in your good Word and faithful promises, so I will devote myself to obey your will and wisdom forever.

**What is the importance of obedience to God?**

# MY STRENGTH

"Be strong and bold; have no fear or dread of them,
because it is the LORD your God who goes with you;
he will not fail you or forsake you."
DEUTERONOMY 31:6 NRSV

You are the source of my strength, God. You support me and
your faithfulness encourages me. I know that you are the
King and ruler over all creation, and you will vindicate your
people in the proper time. I can stand strong against the
enemy who wants to see me destroyed because I know that
you will restore what the enemy seeks to destroy.

May the nations see your sovereign power and humble
themselves before you. May salvation come as your
blessing flows. I will stand strong in the knowledge of your
righteous faithfulness and your great compassion.

**What leads us to fear other people, and how does
faith in God minimize that fear?**

# God Bless You

"The LORD bless you and keep you;
the LORD make his face shine on you and be gracious to you;
the LORD turn his face toward you and give you peace."
NUMBERS 6:24–26 NIV

Oh Lord my God, I long for your presence and to be near to the place of your residence. Draw me close to you so I may live in the shadow of your wings and be strengthened by the water that flows from your throne. Restore to me the joy I had when I first learned of your promises of salvation, and quickly fulfill those promises.

Shine on me, Father; bless me as only you can in abundance of life, grace, and peace and fill the whole earth with these things. Establish your people and make them the joy of all nations. Be pleased with the sacrifice of praise, and come swiftly to your blessed land.

**What is something you need to find peace with that is currently causing conflict?**

# ALL MY DESIRE

Think about the things of heaven, not the things of earth.
COLOSSIANS 3:2 NLT

Lord, I ask you for wisdom from your Spirit as well as strength of focus to remember the blessings you have promised to those who wait patiently for you. I ally myself with you and seek your glory in the eyes of others. You are my great King and I am pleased to serve you.

Help me to serve you in truth and not according to my own interpretations or personal agendas. Let my focus be squarely placed on you and my work be to point others toward you as well. I don't want to be absorbed with a premature fulfillment that really only satisfies my own desire to receive rewards in this life. Lift my eyes to look forward to the things to come.

**What do you think of when you read "things of heaven"?**

# A GIVING HEART

In all things I have shown you that by working hard in this way we must help the weak and remember the words of the Lord Jesus, how he himself said, "It is more blessed to give than to receive."

ACTS 20:35 ESV

Oh Lord, I ask you to help me to be focused outwardly with your good news. Fill me with the desire to dedicate myself to instructing others in your good news and not merely trying to be filled up myself. Let my actions also follow the message of your promises, so I do not hoard what you have given me but share it freely with whomever wishes to receive it.

I know the promises you have set in store for those who persist in good works, so help me to give abundantly to others for their benefit and to strengthen those who are weak and having difficulty in following the path that leads to the fulfillment of your promises. You have—and will—give abundantly from your great wealth; give me the will to do the same. Thank you, my glorious Father!

**A desire to be generous can be found among all different groups of people, but what sets Christian generosity apart from others?**

# It Is You

"The Helper, the Holy Spirit, whom the Father will
send in My name, He will teach you all things,
and bring to your remembrance all that I said to you."
JOHN 14:26 NASB

Father, fill me up with understanding and wisdom so I
may not forget the truth of your good news. Help me to
remember the nature of your good news and the focus that
message creates. Through the work of your Spirit, give me
the strength daily to endure trials and struggles that would
otherwise turn my attention away from you.

You have given me your Scriptures filled with the admonition
to remember your acts of the past to reinvigorate my faith
for your acts of the future. Your promises are the reward
for righteous diligence and the fuel of that diligence is
remembering your faithfulness in the past. Teach me your
ways, oh Lord, and straighten my paths!

**How often has God used your memory of past activity
to encourage you?**

# The Same Wall

I begged the Lord three times to take this problem away from me.
2 Corinthians 12:8 ncv

Father, you are a mighty and majestic God and a good
Father. I am humbled you would even grant me the privilege
to be called by your name. Sustain me in my struggles and
give me the strength I need to endure them with grace and
patience. Help me to submit to the training each difficulty in
my life affords me. Your Spirit and love are enough for me. I
can press through with your encouragement backing me.

Like a proud father, you cheer me on to persevere and strive
with the trials which face me. I will rest in the knowledge
of the confidence you have in your discipline and the
worthy character you are instilling in me. May your glory be
amplified in the midst of these trials as the testimony of your
good news shames the powers and principalities who have
sought your overthrow. I can endure all things for the sake
of your exaltation.

**Do you tend to consider problems opportunities to be
embraced or obstacles to be avoided?**

# SURRENDER AGAIN

My child, give me your heart,
and let your eyes observe my ways.
PROVERBS 23:26 NRSV

My Lord and King, I come before you and swear again my devotion to you and your throne. Show me the desires of your heart and cause the Holy Spirit to wash over me. Teach me the ways of righteousness and I will stand for them. Give me voice to declare the wonder of your great works.

In the power of your Holy Spirit and according to your righteous instruction, cause me to be a true example to others of the nature of your character and let my actions be flavored with the mercy and compassion you have even for your enemies. I will place myself in your care, God, and I will go where you command me. Only have mercy on me and patiently instruct me.

**What results from true surrender to God?**

# COMPASSIONATELY

Jesus, when He came out, saw a great multitude and was moved
with compassion for them, because they were like sheep not
having a shepherd. So He began to teach them many things.

MARK 6:34 NKJV

Lord, you are abundantly compassionate and merciful in the
ways you interact with people. Thank you for your kindness
in taking care of me and offering me a place in your family.
You saw that my way would lead to destruction and, in your
compassion, you reached out to me and offered me life.

Keep me safe in the shelter of your wisdom and teach me
understanding as a shield against the attacks of worldly
powers and the temptations of life. Show me what the path
of righteousness is like and strengthen me to endure it so I
will not wander off the path prematurely. As a good Father,
guide my steps and give me careful instruction in your ways,
to the result of your greater glory.

**How do we incorporate compassion into a message
that includes a rebuke?**

# RESOURCE OF HOPE

Encourage the hearts of your fellow believers and support one
another, just as you have already been doing.
1 THESSALONIANS 5:11 TPT

Father, I desire to be an encourager to others, someone
who instills the courage to continue down this path of faith.
Help me to be a support to the burdens of other people so
they are more able to stand firm in their faith. Fill me with the
wisdom and compassion of the Holy Spirit to be a beacon
of hope to people around me; to be someone with whom
others enjoy approaching and interacting.

I sometimes become too distracted with my own thoughts,
feelings, and burdens and I become closed off to others.
Loosen me up and help me to remain open to people, both
to share myself and welcome their interaction. Father, shine
your light through me so you will be greatly glorified on the
day of your appearing.

**How can we instill hope in others?**

# GRATUITOUS LOVE

By grace you have been saved through faith;
and that not of yourselves, it is the gift of God;
not as a result of works, so that no one may boast.
EPHESIANS 2:8–9 NASB

Almighty God, how magnificent is the fact of your salvation;
how beautiful your offer of good news is to my mind. You
have been gracious in your ways toward me, a man who
has not done anything to deserve your offer of friendship.
You have astounded me with your goodness, for you have
offered to me something I would not offer to my enemies
except for your example.

You, and you only, ought to be praised because of the
goodness you continue to show to the people of the earth—
not only in your persistent offer of friendship but also in the
way you provide for your enemies. You will bring about your
salvation in the earth, restoring all things, by the power of
your Word and you alone will be glorified in that day.

**What is God's motivation for offering salvation
to the world?**

# Exercise in Hope

Be joyful because you have hope. Be patient when trouble comes,
and pray at all times.
ROMANS 12:12 NCV

Lord, you have given me hope beyond my ability to
understand it. I am excited to see the work of your hands
and can hardly contain my anticipation. I trust that you
will accomplish your good will and it will strengthen me
to endure many things in joy because of the surpassing
wonder of what you will bring.

I set my eyes on you and your good promises and I turn my
attention from the things of this life, seeking you and your
righteousness and asking for your continued support. I need
your Spirit to strengthen me because I am weak. You are my
strong tower and I know that you will not leave me ashamed
or alone. I am glad to be called according to your name, my
King; be glorified in me.

**What helps strengthen you to endure troubles when
they come rather than turning from God as some do?**

# COMPARED TO GLORY

I consider that our present sufferings are not worth comparing with the glory that will be revealed in us.

ROMANS 8:18 NIV

How beautiful are the promises you have made to those who put their trust in you, mighty God and King? You are to be exalted and magnified for your sovereign power is great and you will certainly accomplish the things you have promised to do. I am comforted in this life with the idea that, through these trials, you will produce in me a righteous character similar to that of Jesus and will transform my selfish ambition to willful self-sacrifice.

Establish me as a man you are glad to give a place in your kingdom to, but more than that, my heart is strengthened to know that the troubles of this life will not last forever. Your will is to restore and heal, and you will accomplish those things. You will make a world in which righteousness and goodness dwell, and suffering will not be known anymore. Hallelujah!

**How do you find joy in the difficult times of life?**

# Turn Away

No temptation has overtaken you except such as is common to
man; but God is faithful, who will not allow you to be tempted
beyond what you are able, but with the temptation will also make
the way of escape, that you may be able to bear it.

1 Corinthians 10:13 nkjv

Open the door for me, my God, and show me the way
you have provided to escape the temptations of life. I am
thankful that you have provided a mediator who stands at
your right hand to plead for me before you—ne who knows
what it is like to live as a man in this world and has carried
the burdens of life. Hear his intercessions on my behalf
and do not withhold your help from me. I am most grateful
for your attentiveness to my situation and that you have
provided a means of escape.

Teach me your wisdom through the work of your Holy Spirit
and show me your ways that produce righteousness in me.
May my heart be transformed and my desires conformed to
your image. Make your promises real in my understanding
so they strengthen me against the arrows of temptation the
enemy shoots my way, and I will overcome them with your
wisdom and strength.

**How did Jesus overcome the temptations he faced
that are common to man?**

# CONSTANT

This change of plans greatly upset Jonah,
and he became very angry.
JONAH 4:1 NLT

My Lord, increase my understanding so I will be secure in the knowledge of your will. From a worldly perspective, so much of what you do seems contradictory and difficult to understand, but your ways are righteous and good. You are constant in your character and remain faithful and steadfast to your Spirit. You love righteousness and justice and hate wickedness, yet you desire to bless and not curse your creation.

Without wisdom from your instruction, I will be vulnerable to offense at your expense. If I am not taught according to your full counsel, then I will miss what you desire to do. Show forth your righteousness in glory. In the end, I will glorify the incomparable depth of the wisdom of your ways and how you worked all of history to bring about a massive number of people to return to you. Your heart's desire is to see people turn from wickedness. May your efforts prove abundantly successful.

**Have you ever been caught off guard by what appeared to be a change in God's plans for you?**

# My Endurance

Since we are surrounded by so great a cloud of witnesses, let us also lay aside every weight, and sin which clings so closely, and let us run with endurance the race that is set before us.
HEBREWS 12:1 ESV

Strengthen me to run this race of faith, God, for the obstacles laid out before me are many. I see the lives of others who have gone before me and how they sought your good promises and lived their lives in such a way that they might inherit eternal life with you, and I want to join them. Even so, I am weak in so many ways, and staying steady on the path is difficult when the world offers its little enticements.

Conform my will to yours, Lord, so I have the fortitude to say no to the momentary distractions that could so easily derail me and knock me off the path toward life. Help me to focus wholeheartedly on being the man you have called me to be. By the grace of your Holy Spirit, I will run this race of faith in a manner to win it and receive the victor's crown on the day of your glorious appearing.

**What are some weights in your life that cause difficulty in running this race of faith?**

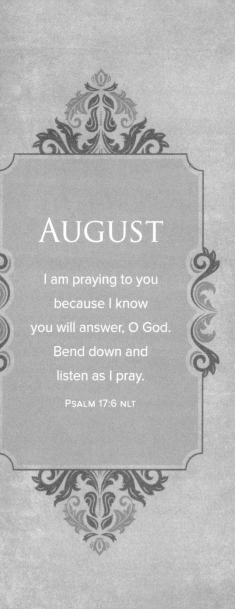

# AUGUST

I am praying to you
because I know
you will answer, O God.
Bend down and
listen as I pray.

PSALM 17:6 NLT

# Lead Me

"Father, if you are willing, take away this cup of suffering.
But do what you want, not what I want."
Luke 22:42 ncv

My Lord, I devote my ways and resources to you. Guide my steps. Send me where you will. I trust in your good wisdom, for you know where history is leading. I know that your promises are true and that you are preparing to restore all things and reward those who have remained faithful to you. Lead me where you choose, and I will go.

Give me the strength to endure the trials and troubles you promised me would happen in this life and with that strength I will go where you take me. I can endure much with your strength and the reminder that the reward is so much greater than the difficulty. Father, it is my fear of death that causes me to falter in this life when faced with difficulty, so help me to remember that death is not the end, for you will make me alive again.

**Can you see God working in your current difficulties?**

# SUFFERING

Heal me, O LORD, and I will be healed;
Save me and I will be saved,
For You are my praise.
JEREMIAH 17:14 NASB

Oh Lord, I need your grace. I need you to do a miracle for me. Sustain me by your powerful works, for I am not able to endure under my own strength. I need your support to help me stand and push forward; do not let me fall and be put to shame. With your strengthening and encouragement from the Holy Spirit, I can endure many things, but I am weak on my own.

I want your will to be done in my life so others will see my testimony—how I endure suffering for the coming prize—and choose to give their hearts to you as well. I put my trust in the salvation you have promised and willingly submit to your orders. Do not withhold from me the provision I need to be able to endure. May you be glorified in this, God, and I will humbly submit to your plan.

**What does it mean to make the Lord your praise?**

# With Patience

If we hope for what we do not see, we wait for it with patience.
ROMANS 8:25 NRSV

Father, I have put my trust in you. I believe your promises. I know you are faithful and that you are strong enough to bring to completion the process you have begun. You began your work all the way back in the garden of Eden when you promised to restore the earth. In this I have put my hope.

When I look at the way you have orchestrated history, the way you have established your chosen people, the way you delivered them from Egypt after 400 years, how you brought forth your Son and provided the way of redemption for your people through his death and resurrection, I know that you will hold fast to your promises. I wait patiently for you to complete your work. Give me the grace to endure this wait with righteousness. Be glorified, oh God, for you are the great King.

**Is it possible to wait with patience for the thing in which you hope if you do not believe the provider is planning to give it to you?**

# WISE ENOUGH

Blessed is the one who perseveres under trial because, having stood the test, that person will receive the crown of life that the Lord has promised to those who love him.

JAMES 1:12 NIV

My God, according to your wisdom, I choose to push forward through trials and troubles, laying down my own attempts at self-preservation in order to receive from you the reward of everlasting life. I ask you for your grace to overcome the temptations of this world that would take me off the righteous path. It is not always easy to convince my body to withstand the difficulties but walking by faith in your promises aids my task.

I know you are faithful and trustworthy, both in your power and desire to accomplish your will, so I ask that you continually remind me of the truth of your power and desire. May your Holy Spirit sustain me with wisdom, courage, signs and memories, and prophetic words that correctly reset my desires when I begin to falter. Thank you for your precious gifts that sustain me on this path. You provide me with all I need to continue. May you fulfill your plans quickly, Lord. May the earth soon be filled with your glory!

**What is wisdom to you?**

# THESE DREAMS

Take delight in the LORD,
and he will give you the desires of your heart.
PSALM 37:4 NRSV

You are good, Lord, and your mercy and provision are incomparable. I desire to see your will done in the earth, so all people will experience the good things you have in store for what you have made. When I consider my own plans for my wellbeing and satisfying my dreams, they pale in comparison to the desires you have in your heart to shower upon your creation.

I turn from my own ambitions and embrace your dreams—dreams you have the power to fulfill—for they are beyond what I could ask or imagine. Even if I were to get the things I want, how would they compare to the benefit of what you have in store for me. You know better what would satisfy me than I do, so I will delight in you and trust you to fulfill your majestic plans.

**Does God fulfill any and all desires when you choose to put your hope in him?**

# AS I LOVE

"To you who are willing to listen, I say, love your enemies!
Do good to those who hate you. Bless those who curse you.
Pray for those who hurt you."
LUKE 6:27–28 NLT

Lord, you do not delight in the destruction of the wicked but desire and rejoice in their turning to you. Mercy inspires you and you love to pour out good gifts. May I be motivated by what motivates you; may my spirit align with yours. Give me compassion for the lost who very often seek to harm me, who do not know any better than to pursue their own good even if it means others may suffer.

Help me to share the good news with those who would take from me. Let the assurance of your abundant provision give me a natural tendency to give even to those who would take by force; let my testimony to them declare my fervent assurance that you will reward all people justly for the works they perform—both good and bad. May my life reflect yours in the treatment of all people.

**Are there people in your life you need to bless even as they curse you?**

# No Reason

God has not given us a spirit of fear,
but of power and of love and of a sound mind.
2 Timothy 1:7 nkjv

Thank you for sharing your Spirit with me, Lord. The Spirit's instruction strengthens me and gives me understanding, showing me the path of righteousness in a world that hates your righteousness. Your Holy Spirit reminds me of your faithfulness and the promises you will fulfill when you come. You spur me on to persist through the attacks that try to scare me into not finishing my walk on this path.

Holy Spirit, strengthen and empower me, giving me the tools I need to resist fear and be courageous in the face of adversity. I can trust you, Father, and I put my hope in you. Continue to help me stay devoted to you and to the renewal of my thoughts, dreams, and desires. May your kingdom come soon, Lord, and your will be done in the earth.

**What is one thing that you find fearsome?**

# HELP ME

"The LORD will fight for you, and you have only to be silent."
EXODUS 14:14 ESV

Father, I need you to help me trust you. You've made me in your image and as such I desire to see justice done. It is difficult for me not to demand justice for myself. I don't want others to take advantage of me or abuse me in some way, but you have called me to follow your example and show restraint. You have said that I should not seek revenge but leave justice to you.

Strengthen my faith to know that if I restrain myself now, you will vindicate me in the day of judgment. Remind me of your mighty works so I may rely on the faithfulness of your judgment. Give me the strength and the self-control to restrain my desire to lash out at those who mistreat me. You will fight on my behalf at the appropriate time. In the meantime, turn the hearts of the wicked around so they seek your glory.

**How hard do you find it to be silent in the face of accusers and abusers?**

# UNSHAKABLE

"The steadfast of mind You will keep in perfect peace,
Because he trusts in You."
ISAIAH 26:3 NASB

You are magnificent, oh God, and worthy of all praise because your faithfulness is beyond compare. What you say you will do. I have no reason to be doubtful of your promises. I glorify your precious name and thank you for steadying my feet with the instruction from your Holy Spirit. Your works from the past remind me of your steadiness and that I can fully trust you to bring about what you have promised. Even in the hardest of times, I can rest assured that you are sovereign.

Remind me each day of your mighty works and your faithful love and kindness for your people so I will be bolstered in faith each day. Give me more understanding of your plan so my faith is increased before you. I know that your plans are certain to be fulfilled and I am filled with peace and joy.

**What causes your mind to become steadfast in your trust of God?**

# GROWING WISER

The wisdom from above is always pure, filled with peace,
considerate and teachable. It is filled with love and never displays
prejudice or hypocrisy in any form.

JAMES 3:17 TPT

Fill me with greater wisdom, Lord, so I may live righteously
before your throne. Increase my understanding of what you
desire for my character, to know what kind of man I ought
to be before you. You have given me Jesus' example as
the Scriptures describe but fill me also with the Holy Spirit
to fully root out wickedness in my character. Establish truth,
peace, and compassion in me as reflections of your gracious
character and help me to be genuine in my motives and the
actions that flow from them.

Your goal is to mold me into someone who serves well
and loves righteously; you want your people to rule the
earth according to the wisdom you have established from
long ago rather than according to the world's wisdom of
selfish exaltation. May it be that I treat others with care and
compassion in my daily life and be willing to serve anyone
according to your incomparable mercy. Fill me with a
steadfast faith so I am capable of flexibility in serving others.

**What does God's wisdom teach you about things in
this life?**

# Enough Today

In all circumstances take up the shield of faith, with which you can
extinguish all the flaming darts of the evil one.
Ephesians 6:16 esv

I echo the request of your disciples, Jesus; increase my faith.
Teach me to truly trust in your faithfulness to keep promises
and to fully hope in the promised restoration of creation
which will come in the appropriate time. The more I look
at my daily circumstances and seek to improve my current
situation, the less I am focused on the day of your coming.
Then I am easily moved to contemplate the temptations
of the world and to falter in my pursuit of your kingdom
and righteousness.

Remind me daily of the promises you have in store for me,
so my strength would be amplified and my will would be
fortified to persevere in the path of righteousness. Help me
to prioritize my time and spend the necessary time warming
up in your Word and in the presence of your encouraging
Spirit. In your strength and power, I will run this race
successfully and fend off the temptations of the evil one.

**What is it about faith that puts out the flaming darts?**

# BURNING JOY

"Go your way, eat the fat and drink sweet wine and send
portions of them to those for whom nothing is prepared,
for this day is holy to our LORD; and do not be grieved,
for the joy of the LORD is your strength."

NEHEMIAH 8:10 NRSV

Lord, how great the celebration will be in the day of your
trumpets' sound, when you call to yourself all the righteous
of the earth and make a proclamation of restoration to
the whole world. In that day there will be rejoicing at your
coming and you will invite us into a magnificent feast. We
will glorify your name in the congregation of the righteous
redeemed from the earth.

For in the day that you blow the trumpet of the archangel,
you will redeem the oppressed and restore health to weary
bones. You are the source of our life and strength and in
you we will rejoice and be made glad. I will lift up a shout
of praise and exalt you, who has fulfilled your promises.
How glorious will that day be? It will be magnificent beyond
words, and the mere thought of it fuels my passion and
desire to live another day for you. Be glorified in all the
earth, Lord, and be exalted in the hearts of men.

**How does your heart swell when you consider the
magnificent promises of God's restoration?**

# EVERYTHING

"You will seek me and find me when you
seek me with all your heart."
JEREMIAH 29:13 NIV

My Lord, you are not impressed with the divided loyalties of a man who tries to satisfy the desires of this life and seek the blessing of the next. Such a person is unstable and will undoubtedly turn back to the siren song of this world. A man cannot serve both the master of this age and the master of the next, and invariably he will be drawn after the more immediate satisfaction offered in this age.

Give me singleness of heart and mind to fully hope in you. I don't want to be turned aside by the anxieties and worries of this life which war against my faith in your goodness. I will seek first your kingdom and put aside the hope of things in this life. Whatever good I receive in this age I will count as nothing to be esteemed but willingly use it so that the good news of your kingdom would be amplified. I trust you for my daily bread, Lord, and eagerly await your coming.

**What are the things in your life that stand in the way of you fully seeking God?**

# HUMBLE SERVANT

"If anyone slaps you on one cheek, offer him the other cheek, too.
If someone takes your coat, do not stop him
from taking your shirt."
LUKE 6:29 NCV

Your mercy and restraint amaze me, God, for I see your generosity abused and your people mistreated, yet you do not strike back in haste. You extend your offer of peace to your enemies and even provide for those who hate you. Your justice is true and certain, so you restrain your wrath for the sake of many who might be saved from it.

May my faith be as strong as I put my trust in your faithfulness. Give me the strength to also show restraint when people try to abuse me and help me to understand that I will receive back in your kingdom what I willingly lose in this age for the sake of you. May my restraint in the face of injustice produce a turning of the heart of the wicked so they may enjoy your mercy. I set my eyes on your promises, Lord, and humbly serve you and your will. Strengthen me to accomplish your righteous task.

**What is the reason for enduring injustice and theft and even giving generously to those who so mistreat you?**

# DISTANT MEANING

You are a chosen generation, a royal priesthood, a holy nation,
His own special people, that you may proclaim the praises
of Him who called you out of darkness into His marvelous light.
1 PETER 2:9 NKJV

Your faithfulness is comforting to me, God. When you give
your Word, you stand by it and fulfill it. I can rest assured
you will destroy the works of the enemy as you promised
because you have stayed faithful to your promises. If you
had reneged or changed the meaning of your words,
who could trust your promises? Instead, you have done
everything you said you would.

Complete your promises to your people so the blessing you
promised would flow from your throne and bring everlasting
life to the world. I have confidence because of your faithful
work with the people you have set apart.

**What are some of the things that give you assurance
that God will actually save you on the day of judgment?**

# EQUAL TRUST

So be strong and courageous,
all you who put your hope in the LORD!
PSALM 31:24 NLT

I trust in you, my God, and I will not be ashamed. You are faithful to exalt those who humbly come before you, recognizing your sovereignty and giving you their devotion. I will persist in my pursuit of your righteous kingdom. According to the Holy Spirit you have shared with me, I will stand steadfast and courageously against the enemy's attempts to cause me to doubt your goodness and the faithfulness of your promises.

You truly are a God of your Word, bringing calamity on the arrogant and wicked whom you have promised to receive it, and rewarding those who have put their hope in you as evidenced by their pursuit of righteousness. Preserve me according to your good will.

**Where is your hope in the Lord to be focused?**

# With Help

I will instruct you and teach you the way you should go;
I will counsel you with my eye upon you.
PSALM 32:8 NRSV

How remarkable and glorious is the Spirit and the Word you have poured out on humanity to show us the righteous path and to guide our steps along it. You have established your people according to your wisdom and have not forgotten the nations of the earth in their rebellion. You reach out to us and offer us your hand of peace, filling us with the desire to seek your face and the coming of your righteous kingdom.

Be persistent in teaching us true wisdom, Lord, and do not leave us to be put to shame. Forgive us our foolishness when we stumble and restore us to our feet for the sake of your great name. I glorify you for your wisdom and mercy to me, Father. I am humbled that you would even consider someone of my position. You are truly majestic and worthy of praise!

**What is the goal of God's instruction?**

# Hope Wins

We also have joy with our troubles, because we know that these troubles produce patience. And patience produces character, and character produces hope.

ROMANS 5:3–4 NCV

Gracious Father, I put my trust in you. I am assured of your good gifts, the gifts you have promised to give to those who turn to you in righteousness, and who make straight their paths before you. You knead me like bread and mold me like clay through the difficulties I face in this life, large and small alike, and this activity produces patience in me as I remember your promises.

You use these times to mold me into the character of your beloved Son, Jesus, and in him—and like him—I will also inherit everlasting life. Lord, fill me with this patience, build in me this character, and help me to wait on you for your timing. I look to you to fulfill your promises to your people, and in the meantime, I find joy in the way that you build discipline in my life.

**How do you think God is building discipline in your life right now?**

# REST AWHILE

All who have entered into God's rest have rested from their
labors, just as God did after creating the world.
HEBREWS 4:10 NLT

My Lord, I am weary and overcome. How long will this last?
When will you complete your work and establish justice and
righteousness in the earth, restoring peace to the creation
you have made? I long to sit and rest awhile, for this struggle
is wearying to the body. Oh, that we might be able to enjoy
your creation together, my King, to rest in the beauty and
completeness of your work.

For now, I strive with the power of your Spirit to overcome
the ways of the world in my own life, to be perfected
through the things I suffer and to struggle against the
enemy's resistance. I am overjoyed that your strength and
might are more than capable of bringing it all to fruition in
your appointed time. May your will be accomplished soon,
my Father, that you may enjoy the fruit of your labors.

**When is the promised rest?**

# IF I QUIT

If we are joined with him in his sufferings, then we will reign
together with him in his triumph. But if we disregard him,
then he will also disregard us.
2 TIMOTHY 2:12 TPT

Great King and Creator of the universe, I pray you give me
the strength to endure your calling to suffer in your name in
this age. As you sustained Jesus to endure the cross, help
me to ignore the momentary relief from difficulty and abuse
I might receive if I were to deny you or repent of my faith.
For the reward you have promised to those who forsake the
satisfaction of this life is immensely greater than either the
reward or the suffering we might find in this life.

What a fearful thing it is to consider you disregarding me,
so I pray you will not take your Holy Spirit from me but daily
restore to me the joy of your promises. Help me to press on
through difficulties; to stop trying to avoid the difficult things
of following you; to embrace the life that comes with being
called by your name. Be magnified and praised by others
because of the testimony you receive from me.

**What does it mean for God to remain faithful in
your faithlessness?**

# LET GO

A time to seek, and a time to lose;
a time to keep, and a time to cast away.
ECCLESIASTES 3:6 NRSV

It's time, oh Lord, to seek what you have in store for the righteous. While the things in my life are shaken to test what is substantial and what is not worthy to be trusted, help me to set my hope in the coming day of your glory. May my storehouse be filled with the treasure that never fades nor goes bad. With the courage and training from your Spirit, I will let go of my need to be satisfied with the things I see around me.

Father, I have trusted so many resources in this life—myself, my job, my government, my family—but you are the one who truly comes through, for your promises will prove to be substantial and real because you have the power to fulfill them. In times of crisis, the resources the world can offer will fail, but you will succeed in establishing your righteous kingdom. It's time for me to fully trust in you.

**Is it time to let go of anything in your life that you have trusted for satisfaction?**

# My Comforter

"Take my yoke upon you. Let me teach you, because I am humble and gentle at heart, and you will find rest for your souls."
MATTHEW 11:29 NLT

According to the nature of your Spirit and kindness, God, teach me your ways that lead to life and rest from a wearying earth. Show me the way of humility and patient restraint that you loved so much in the character of Jesus. May I follow his example as it teaches me the path to everlasting life. You comfort me with righteous teaching and encouraging words in this weary sojourn as I wait for the fulfillment of your blessed promises.

Keep me in your confidence and do not put me to shame but remain patient with me as I learn from you. I am thankful to you for your kindness and favor to me despite my tendency to rebel against you. You are a good Father, providing for all my needs so I may enter your service with confidence and strength.

**How does the Lord teach you?**

# YOUR FAITHFULNESS

My covenant I will not break,
Nor alter the word that has gone out of My lips.
PSALM 89:34 NKJV

Your faithfulness is beyond compare, God, and your commitment to your promises unwavering. Without them, I would have nothing in which to trust, but because I see your trustworthiness I can rest assured that you will certainly bring things to pass that you have said you will do. Father do not let the seed of doubt germinate and grow that says you have changed your purposes because of my actions. Your diligence to chastise your beloved ones will lead to the promise you made that all nations may be blessed.

In what else can I trust if you change the terms of your promises before fulfilling them? Indeed, I may begin to trust in anything my heart can imagine about you if I do not diligently remember that you have set your plans in stone and you will not forsake them. Set my faith firmly in the knowledge of your unwavering devotion.

**What does God's faithfulness encourage you to do?**

# SOME OF HEAVEN

How abundant are the good things
that you have stored up for those who fear you,
that you bestow in the sight of all,
on those who take refuge in you.
PSALM 31:19 NIV

I am amazed at the promise of abundant life and provision
you have established for your children. It defies my
comprehension in this life, where so much of what we get
is the result of toil and struggle, and yet the result is often
so small. You have declared peace and goodness toward
humanity that will give rest for my weary struggles.

As if storing them up, you are refraining from pouring
out your blessings wholesale, but you give me little
tastes of what is to come as a means of encouraging and
strengthening me in my trials. How blessed to receive from
you these nuggets of inspiration that fuel my walk of faith.
I eagerly await the good things you have stored up for
those who fear you.

**What good things do you think the Lord has in store
for you?**

# PROTECT MY HEART

Do not be fooled: "Bad friends will ruin good habits."
1 CORINTHIANS 15:33 NCV

Oh Lord my God, guard my heart and motives from the distractions of this life so that I may remain steadfast on the path toward everlasting life. Surround me with fellow travelers on the path who seriously and joyfully seek the truth of your good news. Help us to better assist each other in following the way of life well.

Lord, I ask you to give me wisdom on how to be able to relate with and reach out to unbelievers who need your good news, and yet also be insulated from the influence of their habits. Instruct me on what Jesus was able to do so that he was known as a "friend of sinners," yet he remained righteous before your eyes. Give me the humility and grace to be able to call people to repentance while not condemning them. I long to be a light of the good news to this world and also remain faithful to you.

**What is the key to interacting with "bad" people in a way that they see you as a friend, yet you aren't drawn to follow them?**

# PAVED ROAD

Without consultation, plans are frustrated,
But with many counselors they succeed.
PROVERBS 15:22 NASB

Father grant me the wisdom and counsel, through your Holy Spirit, to work well before you. You have gifted some to be teachers and some to be prophets and counselors, and I ask you to bring those into my life that I may succeed in the call of righteousness you have given me.

You have not desired that I walk this life alone, and so you have provided a congregation of fellow believers with whom I may walk alongside. Together we may bear with one another and cross the finish line in victory. Reinforce in me the way of life and grant me success as I endeavor to walk that path. I trust in you for your great mercy and the good gifts you give to me to help me along the path. Righteous King, I put my hope in you.

**Who are the counselors you seek to help you make wise decisions?**

# WORDS OF LIFE

"I tell you, on the day of judgment you will have to give an account for every careless word you utter; for by your words you will be justified, and by your words you will be condemned."
MATTHEW 12:36–37 NRSV

My Lord, I ask for your Spirit of wisdom to watch over my words and actions. Help guard my heart and lead me down the correct path. I trust in the sacrifice you have provided for me to cover over my transgression of your commands and the arrogance of my words. May my words and actions be acceptable to you.

Father, forget my careless and useless words and according to your grace do not hold them against me but grant me mercy to enter your presence because of Jesus' sacrifice. I ask you to reward me according to the works my faith produces. May you be exalted because of them. Hallelujah, oh Lord my God!

**How do your words justify you in God's eyes?**

# IT MAKES SENSE

He heals the brokenhearted
and bandages their wounds.
PSALM 147:3 NLT

Lord, you are a good Father and righteous in your ways. You discipline us in mercy and your hand molds our way before us so that we pursue righteousness before you. You heal us and anoint us with your love. You are kind even in discipline, producing righteousness in us. I see my need for your firm hand and am thankful for your work in my life, orchestrating even the difficulties I face into fruit producing character that leads to everlasting life.

Sustain me and fill me with patience as I endure the trials I face with the joy of a beloved son. I will be counted as more than a conqueror when I complete the race you have set before me and stand before you. I will be glad of your lovingkindness in that day.

**What wounds do you need God to heal today?**

# WISE WORDS

Do not believe every spirit, but test the spirits, whether they are of God; because many false prophets have gone out into the world.

1 JOHN 4:1 NKJV

Teach me your ways, glorious God, and give me understanding of your wondrous plans so I am set firmly. Give me the tools I need to discern false spirits who prophesy lies in your name. Set my foundations firmly so I will not be moved from the true Spirit of prophecy. Encourage my spirit and strengthen my will to endure troubles in this life unto the future reward you have in store.

In this age, I will have trouble, but in the next age, your glory will fill the earth as the waters cover the sea. When Jesus appears in the clouds in glory and might, then I will know your deliverance has come, but protect my heart from becoming weak and hoping in a different message.

**What distinguished false prophets from true prophets in the Scriptures?**

# For Good

We are convinced that every detail of our lives is continually woven together to fit into God's perfect plan of bringing good into our lives, for we are his lovers who have been called to fulfill his designed purpose.

ROMANS 8:28 TPT

Good and righteous Father, you are incomparably wise and benevolent. You desire to give good gifts to your people and to establish goodness in the creation. Your Spirit is fully set on providing an abundance of joy, peace, and plenty to your children. You know the heart of humanity and our tendency to worship created things rather than the Creator, so you have provided the means for us to be molded into people worthy to receive the gifts you long to give.

You mold our circumstances around us to increase humility and compassion and cause us to be purified through the troubles this world inevitably brings. You use the hard knocks and rough times to polish us to allow your character to shine through. Your ways are righteous, and you desire to live with righteous people, so you are diligent to train and discipline us for our good. Thank you for working all things together to mold us into your image.

**How does your good Father treat those he considers beloved sons?**

# My Intercessor

In the same way the Spirit also helps our weakness; for we do not know how to pray as we should, but the Spirit Himself intercedes for us with groanings too deep for words.

ROMANS 8:26 NASB

My Lord and God, I exalt you and praise you for you have provided for all my needs. Your Spirit sustains me. You know my deepest needs, things even I do not understand. You desire to fulfill me and to strengthen my weakest parts and you have set your will to accomplish that. Your Spirit, which knows all these innermost needs, cries out to you according to your design and desire to see these things filled up.

Thank you for your desire to do good to me and provide for my deepest needs. I entrust myself to your care. I am relieved to know that I don't have to know all my needs to bring them before you, but you care for me as a father his child.

**Why does the Holy Spirit intercede for you?**

# September

"Keep watch and pray,
so that you will not give
in to temptation.
For the spirit is willing,
but the body is weak!"

MATTHEW 26:41 NLT

# HOPE IN THE LIGHT

"Behold, I am doing a new thing;
now it springs forth, do you not perceive it?
I will make a way in the wilderness
and rivers in the desert."
ISAIAH 43:19 ESV

Thank you, miraculous Lord, for the amazing things you have set out to accomplish. Thank you for your promises to restore the land, to destroy famine and drought, to put an end to suffering and death. You have promised to restore us, and your plans have already begun. You revealed your Son and resurrected him when the enemy attempted to put an end to your plan before it had begun.

Your promises are certain and true, and I put all my hope in you. Restore the dry and thirsty lands; bring life back to dry bones; destroy the wicked oppressor. I long for the day when the nations stream forth to bring glory and honor to you, as you have declared it; the day when your light blots out the very sun in its brilliance.

**What things do you sense in your life that point to God's "new thing"?**

# BRAVE ENOUGH

Lying lips are an abomination to the LORD,
but those who act faithfully are his delight.
PROVERBS 12:22 NRSV

Lord, help me to remain true in my testimony before you. I desire to speak truthfully regarding your good news and to be faithful to the promises you have made. I want to be slow to speak when I am uncertain, rather than quickly blurting out what I think is true. Give me the wisdom to accurately speak of your goodness.

Lord, many who believed they were speaking truth to others were instead pushing a false agenda without even knowing it, but they were too proud to hear the truth. May my heart remain humble before you so I may not seek my own glory and honor among men; I only want to hear the words from you, "Well done, good and faithful servant." Thank you for your Spirit who helps direct me along righteous paths of truth.

**What gives you the strength and courage to speak truth to people who are comfortable with what they know?**

# GREAT THINGS

Using the Scriptures, the person who serves God will be capable,
having all that is needed to do every good work.
2 TIMOTHY 3:17 NCV

My God, the beginning of the Bible is called instruction, and
I ask you to teach me from it the goodness of your plans
and promises. Equip me fully to act according to your will
and the character you desire in a man. You have given me
teaching enough in your Scriptures to know how to behave,
how to love, how to testify.

You have great plans for the earth and its inhabitants—the
righteous remnant of the nations. I am glad to offer my
service, such as it is, to the work you have in store. Give me
what I need to accomplish it in faithfulness. May my offering
be acceptable to you, and your glory increased because of
the testimony of my efforts.

**What are some ways you could accomplish God's good
works today?**

# THE RIGHT PATH

A man's heart plans his way,
But the LORD directs his steps.
PROVERBS 16:9 NKJV

Lead me down the righteous path, my God, and not the path toward destruction. I often desire to chase after the things in this life which make me happy, even if only for a moment, but you have said that path leads to destruction. Give me wisdom to seek after your desires, and to anticipate the joy you have in store for me.

You do not desire a life of boredom and unhappiness for me, but you know that the way I go after adventure and happiness is not righteous. Help me to fulfill your designs for me as a man according to your will and not according to my own. Equip me to perform my acts out of love and care for you and for others rather than selfishly seeking my own desires at cost to others. Direct my steps toward your reward for the righteous, and make my desires align with your own.

**How does God direct the steps of all men?**

# One Thing

"God so loved the world that he gave his one and only Son, that
whoever believes in him shall not perish but have eternal life."
JOHN 3:16 NIV

I am amazed at the lengths you have gone to work
out redemption for your people, oh Lord my God. Your
faithfulness to establish your people in righteousness is
such an encouragement to me. You have declared your
plans from the beginning, and you are diligently bringing
them to fruition.

You have established David as your royal household and
through all the turmoil and needed discipline to chastise
your people, you have brought forth your chosen Son into
the world. Your great and merciful plans are beyond my
understanding, yet you have done all of this because you
desired the nations to turn back to you in faith. I exalt and
glorify your name, oh great God, for your wonderful miracles.

**Do you understand your importance to God through
this Scripture?**

# ONLY HOME

Do not neglect to show hospitality to strangers,
for thereby some have entertained angels unawares.
HEBREWS 13:2 ESV

According to your Spirit, oh Lord, fill me with kindness
and favor toward even the stranger I encounter in life.
Help me to remember that I am only a traveler in this life,
wandering the path until the day you call me home. You
have shown kindness to me and have given me direction
and purpose, so fill me with the same kindness for others.
Help me to care for their needs, to give them a place of
respite and refreshment.

May you be glorified by the nations of the earth when
they see your children motivated to give sacrificially of
themselves for people they do not know. May I be one
of those who gives generously of the resources you
have provided.

**What motivates you to be hospitable?**

# ONLY LOVE

Love each other with genuine affection,
and take delight in honoring each other.
ROMANS 12:10 NLT

I love living in fellowship with your children, God, so we can encourage each other and accompany one another along this path toward everlasting life. I am blessed to know the people of God and to seek you together with them, to experience camaraderie, and to serve in righteous commitment. You have said the world would know us by the way we treat each other, giving generously to each other and not seeking repayment, supporting and caring for each other's wellbeing.

Fill me with this love for your family and give me the wisdom to know how to best serve them and be open to their service. Build the community of believers together through our shared experience. May my heart of compassion extend far and wide. Help me to honor my brothers in foreign countries who serve you in ways I cannot even imagine. Father, most of all, be glorified in our acts of kindness and faithful love one to another.

**How have you been shown care by the community of believers?**

# MORE LIKE YOU

I pray with great faith for you, because I'm fully convinced that the
One who began this glorious work in you will faithfully continue
the process of maturing you and will put his finishing touches
to it until the unveiling of our Lord Jesus Christ!

PHILIPPIANS 1:6 TPT

Oh Father, you are good in your promises and in the work
you are doing in the earth. Thank you for drawing me
near to you with your offer of peace and for treating me
like your child, for you teach me diligently and discipline
me faithfully. You have desired righteous offspring who
would administrate your earthly creation with honor and
compassion, taking care to protect it rather than exploit it.
Help me to recognize the difference and to learn to care
for others.

You are diligent and faithful in your kindness, mercy, and
patience, and I am humbled by your care. Who am I that the
King of the universe would care for my specific wellbeing
and would take an interest in my life? Yet you have done so
with passion and faithfulness. I am forever grateful to you
and your persistent work to make me worthy of the gifts you
intend to give me. Be blessed and glorified, Lord.

**What is the glorious work that God begins in the life of
a believer?**

# ADVERSITY

"My grace is sufficient for you, for power is perfected in weakness." Most gladly, therefore, I will rather boast about my weaknesses, so that the power of Christ may dwell in me.
2 CORINTHIANS 12:9 NASB

Strengthen me according to the wisdom and knowledge of your Holy Spirit so I will be able to stand firm in adversity. I am weak, Lord, and I need your encouragement to press through adversity. Like a football player who sees the vision of championships won and it fuels him to endure the pain of training, so I seek greater inspiration to fuel me to press through the trials and troubles of life and be made a faithful and vibrant man in your sight.

Your power is made known in the earth when you take the least desirable from the nations and you overcome worldliness in them where they are most vulnerable. Then your name is exalted before the powers and principalities you established, and you validate your wisdom before them. I put my trust in you, God, to sustain me despite my weakness. You are a kind and good King, and I am honored to call you my Father.

**How do you benefit by admitting your weakness?**

# LOVE NEVER ENDS

A thousand years in your sight
are like a day that has just gone by,
or like a watch in the night.
PSALM 90:4 NIV

Lord, your faithfulness continues for all time; you will not turn your back on what you have determined to sustain. You have established the earth in your wisdom and called it good and set humanity over it as your governor; therefore, you will remain faithful to us forever.

You are faithful and true to your commitments, and you have promised to lovingly heal our wounds. You are kind and compassionate to what you have made. You will take your stand to overthrow oppression and wickedness, the fruit of evil and rebellion, and you will establish righteousness for all who have put their trust in you, for you love those who love you.

**What does it mean to love God?**

# THE SAME HANDS

"You have also given me the shield of Your salvation;
your gentleness has made me great."

2 SAMUEL 22:36 NKJV

Father, teach me the wisdom of your ways so I may teach
it to others, for your glory is wonderful. You are the great
King and you watch over the world in your sovereign power.
Through you comes both justice and mercy, blessing and
curse, exaltation and destruction; yet, you are consistent in
your ways.

You establish the righteous perpetually, but the wicked you
cast down. You discipline the people you love, and you heal
their wounds. In your justice you punish the wicked for the
way they have caused trouble and pain, but in your mercy
you offer them a chance to turn away from their evil ways
and be joined with the righteous. You delight in destroying
wickedness, but you do not relish the thought of destroying
the wicked. You will give the righteous victory over their
enemies, but you offer a chance to those enemies to switch
sides. You are the God who makes all of this come to pass
and I will exalt your name forever.

**How has God's gentleness made you great?**

# No Words

They sat on the ground with him for seven days and seven nights.
No one said a word to him, because they saw how great
his suffering was.

JOB 2:13 NIV

Oh Father, sustain me in the day of mourning, in the day
when I am overwhelmed with the sin and struggle of this life,
with the sickness and death that surround and engulf me. I
am not able to express the depth of my anguish. How long
can you let this go on? How long will you withhold justice
from the earth? I am unable to endure the pain and agony
that ravages my senses; uphold me with the power of your
Holy Spirit.

Search the depths of my heart, God, and comfort me. Hear
the petitions I don't even know how to articulate and cry
out on my behalf. May my requests be heard at your altar
as you renew my strength. Refresh the earth in your great
wisdom and bring healing to the broken and wounded.
Provide for the poor and sustain the needy. Give them hope
in your goodness. I will stand before you and tell of your
wonderful kindness.

**What can premature words in the face of pain
accomplish?**

# WHEN GLORY COMES

We thank God! He gives us the victory
through our Lord Jesus Christ.
1 CORINTHIANS 15:57 NCV

Oh, how excited I am for your arrival, Lord! To hear the trumpet announcing the victory, raising us all in glory to join you for the celebration feast. Your kingdom will have no end and your righteous King will be enthroned, governing the world in righteousness and peace, pouring forth blessing that will be the healing of the nations.

You are glorious, for the wisdom of your plans and the way you are bringing them to fruition. I am ever grateful for the mercy you have given that saves a sinner like me. Keep my path straight and give me strength to remain faithful to it so I will reach the day of salvation with confidence and certainty, not because I deserve it but because you have desired to give the gift to those who love and follow you with their whole being. Blessed are you above all else, for no one and nothing is like you.

**Do you ever find yourself living more for what the Lord can do for you now than hoping in the reward to come?**

# BROUGHT NEAR

Bear one another's burdens, and thereby fulfill the law of Christ.
GALATIANS 6:2 NASB

Jesus, you said that the second greatest commandment is to love one another as ourselves which is the heart of the Law. Teach me to exhibit this outward expression to others and empathize with their experience. I know the kind of care I want in my times of trouble, stress, and weakness, so help me to treat others who face the same trials with the same care. I will be a support to my brother, recognizing that I am no better than him even if I am currently free from the struggle he faces.

Give me soothing words that strengthen and encourage, not words that destroy the spirit or bring condemnation. May my actions toward others be flavored with mercy so they are restored when they have fallen. You have given me favor I do not deserve, Father; now help me to pour out that favor to my brother.

**How can you bear someone else's burden?**

# ABBA

Whoever spares the rod hates his son,
but he who loves him is diligent to discipline him.
PROVERBS 13:24 ESV

Thank you, Father, for your persistence to mold me. You show me your love and compassion through the way you will not leave me alone. You draw me back and will not let me falter for good. Instead, you steady my feet and strengthen what is weak in my character. Though the process is hard, you are diligent to make sure I learn the ways of righteousness and am strong enough to walk this path.

You have taken me and given me a place among your people; I am secure. I know your care for me and am humbled that you would count me as one of your own. I am grateful for what you are building in me and how you are molding me into a man of righteousness, one worthy to receive the reward you will give. I glorify you with all my heart, gracious Father.

**As a good Father who disciplines, what kinds of things does God do to discipline you?**

# ACCESS TO WISDOM

"Call to me and I will answer you, and will tell you great and
hidden things that you have not known."
JEREMIAH 33:3 NRSV

Father let me drink freely of your Spirit, be filled with
understanding, and be encouraged with great things that
are beyond my usual comprehension. Fill me with wisdom
and knowledge that strengthen my hope in the day of your
appearing and compel me to exalt you while humbling
myself at your feet. You are the great God and Father of
all the earth, who provides for it and cares for all you
have made.

You will not subject your creation to futility and wicked kings
forever but will one day stand forth and put an end to the
wicked ways of the worldly powers who have forgotten their
place or willfully rebel against your rule. In your great power,
fill me with faith to stand fast in the face of great opposition
and to remain steady in my allegiance to your throne. Thank
you for enlightening me with instruction in truth for my
former ways would lead merely to destruction.

**What is the goal of godly wisdom?**

# You Alone

No one is holy like the LORD!
There is no one besides you;
there is no Rock like our God.
1 SAMUEL 2:2 NLT

You are great among all the kings and gods of the nations, oh Lord! You have established the world in all its inherent systems, creating them according to your great wisdom. You have established a hierarchy of power and authority and have set your creatures into those positions; yet, no matter how they use their authority, you orchestrate the events to accomplish your purposes.

All beings are subject to you, oh God, regardless of what they think or believe about you, and your plans are beyond thwarting. I will put my trust and hope in you. May the nations and all their people recognize your sovereignty so they may be saved in the day of your coming. Exalt your name in the eyes of the nations so we may survive the fire of your coming. No one is like you, Lord!

**Do you sometimes trust in other sources of stability?**

# EVERY CHANCE

"I am the Way, I am the Truth, and I am the Life.
No one comes next to the Father except through
union with me. To know me is to know my Father too."
JOHN 14:6 TPT

Oh Father, you sent Jesus into the world to show us what
kind of person you are. We can gain insight into you through
growing in the knowledge of Jesus' character. His Spirit
was in alignment with yours. Father, I ask you to help this
character grow within me. May those who meet me come
to grow in their understanding of you and your promises
as they get to know me and see the way that your Spirit is
producing fruit in my life.

I wish—like Paul—to be one who fills up, through my own
testimony, what is lacking for others in their understanding
of your graciousness and character in every instance in life.
Help me to be a strong witness of what you are like until the
day when you come and reveal all in power and glory.

**What are some things that Jesus is calling you to
join him in?**

# DELIGHT IN WEAKNESS

That is why, for Christ's sake, I delight in weaknesses,
in insults, in hardships, in persecutions, in difficulties.
For when I am weak, then I am strong.
2 CORINTHIANS 12:10 NIV

Father, I need your help. I need your strength; I need your support. I am weak despite all my efforts to be strong, to be enough. I falter. But thank you, my God, that you use these times to show forth your own strength. Help me to embrace my weakness and turn my thoughts to how to seek your strength rather than bolster my own abilities.

You uphold the weak and exalt the humble. You give grace to those who know their faults and confess them readily. May I be one who stands before you unashamed of my weaknesses, ready to have you glorified through them. Help me to find joy in the things I am not sufficient to endure because I know that you are exalted most when I am least capable.

**Do you find it difficult to be comfortable with your weaknesses? Why or why not?**

# All Honor

The answer is, if you eat or drink, or if you do anything,
do it all for the glory of God.
1 CORINTHIANS 10:31 NCV

Glorious God, you are worthy of all praise and glory. You are to be praised above all things and worshiped in all things. Your majesty fills the whole earth, and its magnificence shall be evident to all people.

Lord, help me to be the type of example that does not cause others to divide their loyalties with you. I wish them to know what it truly means to worship the one God above all, and to do so in the manner you have called us. I desire to live so that you, and no other, are glorified in the things I do. May I not cause someone to stumble into sin because of the things I do so they may glorify you.

**How can you bring glory to God in all the things that you do?**

# Just Us

The faith which you have, have as your own conviction
before God. Happy is he who does not condemn
himself in what he approves.

ROMANS 14:22 NASB

Deal with me according to my actions, Father, and help me not to compare myself with others. You know the plans you have established, and you know the state of my heart and desires. According to your Spirit, cleanse me from the things I need washed and give me understanding from your instruction.

Help me to be careful before others that I do not lead them astray by anything I do, giving you the space to address them in the way they need. I pray I would not be a stumbling block for others causing them to believe it is ok to partake in things that are sinful and still be in good standing with you.

**How can you avoid causing others to believe it is ok to sin even when you don't believe the same thing is sinful?**

# POWERFUL PRESENCE

You make known to me the path of life;
in your presence there is fullness of joy;
at your right hand are pleasures forevermore.

PSALM 16:11 ESV

You are so good, God, in how you provide for my every need and make available to me the tools necessary to walk rightly in faith. I am awe-inspired that you consider even the smallest details of my life and orchestrate training that targets all my needs. You mold me according to the image of Jesus and encourage me with the certainty of your faithfulness.

How wonderful it is that even when life presents anxious times and sad circumstances, my faith in the hope of your restoration gives me the strength to face those times with joy that overcomes. May your will be accomplished in the earth, God.

**How can you have joy in even the darkest circumstances in life? What makes it all worth it?**

# LIFE OF INTEGRITY

For our sake he made him to be sin who knew no sin, so that in him we might become the righteousness of God.
2 CORINTHIANS 5:21 NRSV

God, the way you have worked out salvation for the world is amazing! Though you had previously given your instruction to the world, you then provided the epitome of an example to us in the very life of Jesus. He showed us the way, teaching the way of truth and laying down his life in the face of injustice so that even your enemies might be preserved from judgment. You led him to give of himself in the punishment that sin requires though he did not deserve it so that we who are unworthy of your favor might have every tool available to equip us to live righteously before you and inherit the awesome reward you have stored.

Preserve my life, Lord, not so I never face trouble but so the character and integrity of a life righteously lived in the face of any adversity might be established in me. Produce in me the self-sacrificial character of Jesus. I want to be a true witness of your goodness, God.

**How do you become the righteousness of God?**

# WHAT I WOULD DO

"If the world hates you, remember that it hated me first."
JOHN 15:18 NLT

My Lord and King, why do the nations work so hard to thwart your plans and to prevent you from blessing the earth? Why do people seem to hate you so much? Why is it so hard for us to see that you have the best in mind for all your creation? I have often been drawn away to seek after my own comfort. So often that leads to abuse and corruption against others, yet in my haste and selfish designs, I do not even realize the damage I do. Forgive me for the times I have done this and give me compassion for others who do not see the true effects of their corrupted ways.

Fill me with your desire to see all people turn from their own determination of what is good and evil to submit to your truth. I set my eyes on your promises and patiently await them. May the nations turn to your mercy before the great and terrible day of your judgment.

**What caused you to turn from hatred of God's ways to desire to see them fulfilled?**

# GREATER IMPACT

Commit your work to the LORD,
and your plans will be established.
PROVERBS 16:3 NKJV

Oh Lord, I give my allegiance to you and choose to
follow your ways. I devote my work to follow the path of
righteousness so what I choose to work at in life will align
with your goals and purposes. Establish this work according
to your grace and accomplish the promises you have made
to me.

You have chosen the earth as the place you are working
out redemption, and I long to see and participate in the
promises you have made. Help me to desire your good
news with everything I have and to find my motivation in
pointing people you. Be magnified in the earth, Lord.

**What does it mean to commit your work to the Lord?**

# THE SOURCE

All praise to God, the Father of our Lord Jesus Christ.
God is our merciful Father and the source of all comfort.
2 CORINTHIANS 1:3 NLT

What do I have that you did not provide, God? Everything from the air I breathe to the materials for the clothes I wear, and even my body are all here because of your work and provision. Therefore, I put my trust in you to provide for all my needs, and I will recognize that when I do not receive what I think I need, that is also your provision.

You do not only provide for the sake of my comfort but also for the sake of my character and for the sake of others' salvation. Your wisdom is incomparable, and I know that you are inclined to do what is good for those who call you their Father. I will trust in the path you lead me down, and I will be patient to receive the ultimate comfort and rest you have promised to those who diligently seek righteousness before you.

**What differentiates the comfort that comes from God and the comfort you seek for yourself?**

# ANCHORED

Let him ask in faith, with no doubting, for he who doubts is like a
wave of the sea driven and tossed by the wind.
JAMES 1:6 NKJV

Father, I ask you to increase my faith and to help me place
my hope completely in the day that you bring your reward
with you. Solidify my heart in the promises of your good
news and loving faithfulness. Help me to stop wavering
between the temporary comforts of this life and the
everlasting beauty of the next life.

I want my heart to be fully anchored in the desires of your
will so the things I ask for and seek will be fully assured.
You will lift up my requests and bring them to pass because
it will delight you to provide them. Be glorified before the
nations of the earth and let all people come to recognize
your goodness.

**What does it mean to be a double-minded man? How
is it related to doubting the good news?**

# Meet Me

It is not yet time for the message to come true, but that time is coming soon; the message will come true. It may seem like a long time, but be patient and wait for it, because it will surely come; it will not be delayed.

HABAKKUK 2:3 NCV

Increase my endurance before you, Lord, so I may continue to run this race of faith through time and trouble. Give me strength so I will not turn back at the apparent slowness I perceive in the fulfillment of your promises. I will wait for you to establish your righteousness in the earth because you are certain to establish it in its appropriate time.

Equip me with patient endurance that will permit me to submit to the mercy you are extending. Fill me with your compassion for the wicked as well as the poor and oppressed to see many people put their trust in your coming salvation and your house be filled at the celebratory feast you are preparing.

**Why is it important for you to exhibit patience in the face of God's "slow" fulfillment?**

# STAYING FOCUSED

Love is patient, love is kind. It does not envy,
it does not boast, it is not proud.

1 CORINTHIANS 13:4 NIV

Conform my character to yours, God, and clarify the image of Jesus that I am reflecting according to the power of your Holy Spirit in me. May my ways be filled with kindness and compassion just as Jesus was patient and kind with those who came to him. Give me a strong love for your Word and the fulfillment of your glory in the earth so I may extend your offer of peace to any and all I encounter.

God, your willingness to endure the wickedness and destruction wrought by evil men in the earth for the sake of establishing your peace with as many as possible is mind-blowing. I know that without the help of your Spirit, I would be unable to endure even the slightest infractions against my family and possessions; yet, you have endured millennia of transgressions and the brutal murder of your Son in order to extend a treaty of peace to the world. May your efforts prove utterly fruitful, and may my life reflect your character.

**How do you stay focused on the good news in the clamor of the world's distractions?**

# RECONCILIATION

"My people who are called by My name humble themselves and pray and seek My face and turn from their wicked ways, then I will hear from heaven, will forgive their sin and will heal their land."

2 CHRONICLES 7:14 NASB

Oh Lord, hurry to fulfill your promises of reconciliation and restoration. You have established your plan to draw people back to yourself and to turn from the wickedness we so readily pursue. Father, I confess to you my disobedience; I confess that I have pursued the things of this life and the comforts it provides, and I have not sought after your righteousness.

Please forgive these things in me, and in my people. Hear our cry for restoration and reconciliation and remember your promise to Adam and Eve to overthrow the curse and the authority of the enemy. Establish your righteous kingdom in the earth and heal the land. May your name and yours alone be exalted in all the earth, and may all nations repent before you.

**What does God mean by healing the land?**

# OCTOBER

Answer me when
I pray to you,
my God who does
what is right.
Make things easier for me
when I am in trouble.
Have mercy on me
and hear my prayer.

PSALM 4:1 NCV

# GUARD MY HEART

Set your minds on things that are above,
not on things that are on earth.
COLOSSIANS 3:2 NASB

My God, you have declared your righteousness and faithful
promises from the heavenly throne room; may my longing
be in line with these things. I do not want to be overcome
with desire for the things with which the world tries to
distract me. The world often places things before me that
you have established for good and worthy purposes, yet my
heart seeks after them in a wrong way.

In the power of the Holy Spirit, mold my heart to long for
righteous activity and not in the longing of people who
have no hope for a life beyond this one. Guard my thoughts
and desires and channel them according to your righteous
intention. May my hope be firmly rooted in the promises you
have ordained.

**What are the "things that are above"?**

# TEMPORARY

We do not look at the things which are seen, but at the things
which are not seen. For the things which are seen are temporary,
but the things which are not seen are eternal.

2 CORINTHIANS 4:18 NKJV

Father God, you are glorious in your ways and marvelous in
your great promises. The world acts as if it will continue as
it does for as long as possible, but you have set a day when
you will judge the righteous and the wicked. I long for the
day when disease, famine, drought, abuse, and disaster are
a thing of the past, but for now I am surrounded by it.

Even so, I do not let these things destroy my hope and joy.
I know that these things will not last; they are temporary as
are so many of the fleeting attempts to find happiness to
which the world devotes itself. Lord, guard me against falling
into the despair that leads the world to chase things that
won't last and strengthen me in my resolve to run after your
good promises.

**What eternal things are you setting your heart on
right now?**

# EMPATHY

If one part suffers, every part suffers with it;
if one part is honored, every part rejoices with it.
1 CORINTHIANS 12:26 NIV

Father God, fix me with a unified hope in the one true hope of your restoration and help me to walk with others along the path to that glorious day. Help me to bear the burdens of my fellow travelers, mourning with them in sorrow and rejoicing with them in even the smallest victories along the path.

I am not a lone ranger walking this path without a companion, but you have ordained that many would walk this path together to encourage and support each other in keeping a straight course. Fill me with your compassion and care for your people. Behold how good it is to dwell with your righteous people in unity. I am thankful for your great mercy to provide fellowship in the good and the bad of traveling through this age. You are a good Father and caring provider.

**What creates the unity of the body of believers producing the above camaraderie?**

# My Name

See, I have written your name on my hand.
Jerusalem, I always think about your walls.
ISAIAH 49:16 NCV

Father, you never, ever forsake your people. Your righteous faithfulness would not permit you to do so, and you have filled your plans with the joy of blessing your people. May I be fortunate enough to be counted among the righteous who are blessed in your work. I am humbled and greatly honored that you have offered your precious salvation to me.

Fulfill your promises to establish and restore your people and fill the earth with the righteous you have promised to exalt. May your joy be filled full in all the earth as your name is vindicated and you show your true love and kindness to the people the world has hated. I long for the day when you are finally satisfied in your mighty work.

**How comforting is it to know that God remembers his promises to you?**

# JOY IS MEDICINE

A joyful, cheerful heart brings healing to both body and soul.
But the one whose heart is crushed
struggles with sickness and depression.
PROVERBS 17:22 TPT

Thank you, Father, for your good news, in which anticipation for its fulfillment brings such a great amount of joy. Fill me with wonder and imagination concerning the reality of your promises and feed my joy according to the working of your Holy Spirit. Such joy brings vitality to me and causes others to wonder at my exalted spirits.

I am so grateful that you have promised your forgiveness. How can I not rejoice in the knowledge that you will not hold my faults against me? I will share my joy with others; bring the healing with you when you come and establish your righteous goodness in all the earth.

**To what extent has God worked to bring joy to your soul?**

# GET IT RIGHT

"Where your treasure is, there will your heart be also."
LUKE 12:34 ESV

My Lord, when I consider your creation and how you made humanity, you intended for us to live forever with you working together in governance of the earth. When we corrupted ourselves and began to follow the counsel of the enemy, you established a temporary condition on the earth in which your creation, including us, would be subject to death. You promised that, in time, you would bring forth a deliverer who would restore the creation.

So now, ever since the first declaration of your good news, the world has been divided by those who believe you that these circumstances are temporary and those who do not believe that you will restore. They are both characterized by how we live in this time, whether living to maximize our experience now—knowing they will die—or willing to largely ignore what can be gained temporarily for what will be possessed forever. What good does it do me to gain more in this life while sacrificing what you offer in the next? I will choose to serve you, God, and hope in your good will.

**What tools does God give to combat the temptation to settle for this life?**

# Not Worried

Anxiety weighs down the human heart,
but a good word cheers it up.
PROVERBS 12:25 NRSV

Oh God, your good news inspires me, and I am overjoyed. Though my life is filled with uncertainty and my circumstances frequently seem shaky, yet the knowledge that you are going to restore all things and fulfill everyone's needs lifts my spirits. I know I will face struggles, sometimes intense trouble, but that will not be the end for me. You are watching and working to draw humanity to your banner, to fill your house with worshipers who will glorify you in the earth and will wait on your faithful promises.

Together, we turn from the anxious times of the world and encourage each other with reminders of your faithfulness and compassion. The stories of your goodness reinvigorate my faith each day. Continue to strengthen me with your Spirit's instruction and words of knowledge and understanding. They are like the sun shining through the clouds on a dreary day.

**What do you worry about from day to day, and how could God help you with that worry?**

# WEALTH OF CHARACTER

Choose a good reputation over great riches;
being held in high esteem is better than silver or gold.
PROVERBS 22:1 NLT

Your Word tells me that I should use the riches I gain in this life to make friends so that I will have much companionship in the life to come. As I put aside satisfying my own desires for wealth and power and seek instead your kingdom and the character that comes from following your path, I look forward to impacting people with your message.

What testimony would I have if my desires are so obviously motivated by selfish pursuits in this world like everyone else? I ask you to set me apart from the crowd in the way I can be trusted and the way I care for others, showing compassion to the broken, mercy to my enemies, and provision to the needy. May this be a testimony of your love, and may it draw many others to you.

**What makes a good reputation better than silver or gold?**

# CALL TO LOVE

Do not rejoice when your enemy falls,
And do not let your heart be glad when he stumbles.
PROVERBS 24:17 NKJV

Lord, I long for justice to prevail in the earth and for your righteous rulership to bring goodness and peace to earth. I pray for humility and contrition on the part of those who despitefully act in rebellion against your ways just as you also offered peace to me though I was not your friend.

May the stumbling of the proud and arrogant cause them to see their error and turn to your gracious mercy. In that I will rejoice, to see another member of your coming kingdom come from the population of those consigned to destruction. Help me to have the compassion and humility to offer a hand of assistance to my enemy who stumbles, to the end that he become my friend.

**Does your heart have compassion for your enemies to the point of dying for them?**

# Strength Revealed

Yours, LORD, is the greatness and the power
and the glory and the majesty and the splendor,
for everything in heaven and earth is yours.
1 CHRONICLES 29:11 NIV

Lord, when I see the way you work in the earth to this day, I am inspired to hope more deeply in the day when you will fully reveal your arm to the world and show forth your majestic strength. I am astounded by the small signs of remembrance you set forth; how much more amazing will your grand finale be? You have created all things and sustain them by your might, and you set up nations and kingdoms and you tear them down.

You orchestrate the circumstances of the earth to produce the effect you desire. Your miraculous acts are fantastic and encouraging, and they strengthen me to trust the validity of your great promises. Like the thrill of the crowd when a runner breaks into the open field, I cheer on the day in which you will reveal your majesty. Everything belongs to you, God, and I long for the day when all of it will submit to your glory.

**How thrilling is it to consider the day that God finally reveals the fullness of his majesty?**

# THE ONLY JUDGE

God is the only Lawmaker and Judge. He is the only One who can save and destroy. So it is not right for you to judge your neighbor.
JAMES 4:12 NCV

Righteous King, I anxiously await the day when you will establish justice and righteous rulership in the earth. You are the righteous judge and you will execute justice in full wisdom because you see to the very hearts of people and you know what motivates us in our innermost secret places. You have established your righteous commands.

May it be that I declare your coming judgment and emphasize the mercy you offer. Help me to have a kind and compassionate attitude toward others, remembering my own faults and selfish ways. You have shown me great mercy, Lord, and I ask that you help me to reflect that mercy to others. Shine the polish on the image I am to bear, Father, and help me to show a gracious countenance to those who seek your kingdom. You are a good God; you are a good King; you are a good judge; I trust your wise decisions.

**How does God call someone to turn from wickedness and also not judge them?**

# FAITHFUL IN LITTLE

"He who is faithful in a very little thing is faithful also in much;
and he who is unrighteous in a very little thing
is unrighteous also in much."

LUKE 16:10 NASB

Father, teach me to be faithful with the things I have, to treat them with respect, and to honor you with the things I do. I wish to be a faithful servant who can be trusted to devote himself to you in all things. Fill me with wisdom to find motivation in each task I face and to do all things as though I were doing them for you. May my eyes be fixed on your righteousness and mercy to motivate me to take care with the things I have been given.

You are a wise Father who sees the end from the beginning and has insight into the hearts of men. You see our infatuation with great plans and large-scale accomplishments, but you know that we need to be trained first. You entrust us with small tasks to test our abilities and to see our level of commitment. Help me to be faithful to you in all things, Father, and to value the instruction you give, not becoming distracted with the large plans, but being faithful exactly where you have put me.

**Do you find it difficult to remain faithful in small things especially when they don't seem that important?**

# HONEST WORSHIP

Oh come, let us worship and bow down;
let us kneel before the LORD, our Maker!
PSALM 95:6 ESV

You are the King of all kings, the God of all gods, the Creator of all creatures, and your sovereign will is abundantly good! I exalt you, Lord, for your majestic works and your compassionate mercy are beyond understanding. Your creation rightfully praises you for you are its source and have established its righteous paths.

Renew your creation and establish it in full goodness and peace; destroy the wicked from its midst and show forth your majestic power. You will accomplish your divine decrees from ancient times. You and only you will receive glory in that day, and all the earth will be glad.

**What distinguishes honest worship from false worship?**

# SHOW ME BEAUTY

I praise you, for I am fearfully and wonderfully made.
Wonderful are your works; that I know very well.
PSALM 139:14 NRSV

Lord, I pray that you would mold me in such a way that I can see beauty where I otherwise wouldn't. Train my eyes to look for the wonder of your creation and to be sensitive to hidden treasures within people. Your creation is good and wondrous; let my mind focus on the wonder—on anything good. Fill me with your Spirit to help me to think and see as you do.

May my heart be honorable and devoted to what is good and beautiful in your creation. I am comforted and my spirits are lightened when I can enjoy the beauty of your work. A mountain storm, colorful sunsets, the nighttime sky, a person helping another in need: these all bring joy to my heart and longing for the day when you reveal the fullness of your creation's beauty. Thank you for your creative works and for the beauty of the earth you have made.

**How does the beauty of God's creation affect
your spirits?**

# BOLD CONFIDENCE

It is not that we think we are qualified to do anything on our own.
Our qualification comes from God.
2 CORINTHIANS 3:5 NLT

Father, as I put my faith and trust in you, anticipating your work in my life to transform my worldly character into the image of Jesus, I am filled with appreciation for the way you make me ready to live appropriately. You give me righteous teaching that flows from your wisdom, and you give me compassionate mercy that flows from your lovingkindness. I have great confidence in the paths you have established to prepare me to walk out my faith.

You have filled me with assurance because of the testimony of so many other faithful people who have lived before me, and you have reinforced it with the powerful work of your Holy Spirit in encouraging words of wisdom and knowledge and samples of your wondrous power. I know that all these flow from your throne through your Spirit because on my own I am not worthy of the good things you have promised to those who follow you. You are my strength; I give honor to you.

**Does your confidence come merely from declaring your faith, or do you have it because of the fruit of that declaration? What is the fruit?**

# REDEMPTION

"As for you, you meant evil against me; but God meant it for good,
in order to bring it about as it is this day,
to save many people alive."

GENESIS 50:20 NKJV

Good King, I am awestruck with the unfathomable ways
you have conceived to orchestrate salvation for your
people and others from all nations. You are masterful in
the way you work any situation into a way to produce
good circumstances down the line as well as building the
character of your people through it all.

You are a magnificent strategist and I am completely
confident to entrust you with the circumstances of my life.
Have your way in me, Lord, and use me for the purposes
you have in store. I will glorify you for the way you use even
the plans of your enemies to thwart their goals. What power
can they have over me that you won't overthrow?

**How have even the dark parts of your experience
ended up profitable for God's purposes in you? How
does that knowledge affect the way you remember or
heal from the experience?**

# I HAVE FAITH

Faith is confidence in what we hope for
and assurance about what we do not see.
HEBREWS 11:1 NIV

Father, you are wondrous in your ways and in the wisdom you have set forth. Faith in you is not blind, for you have shown proof of your faithfulness to countless people over the generations of humanity. You have established your people and have upheld them, protecting them even from extinction. You have performed countless miracles and changed numerous lives.

I am confident you will faithfully fulfill your promises to destroy the authority of the enemy and restore the goodness of the earth. You will save the faithful and righteous among the nations who long for you. My trust and hope are well-founded, and I have certainty of your fulfillment even though I do not yet see your promises fulfilled. I have faith in you, great King!

**What supports your faith in God?**

# GOODNESS ITSELF

Let love be genuine. Abhor what is evil; hold fast to what is good.
ROMANS 12:9 ESV

Father help me to love others righteously and not be hypocritical in my motives toward them. May my focus be like yours and my desire be to see people saved. Help me to be kind to the oppressed in the message of your good news regarding repentance and not judgmental regarding the wickedness and evil I encounter.

According to your Spirit, help my heart remain soft toward others and not be hardened even when I face harshness and criticism. I ask for your mercy to flow from me rather than self-preservation and protection. May my words reflect your gentleness when appropriate, and speak forcefully when necessary but always with the compassion you possess. Father, you are the epitome of love; shine that love through me.

**What is genuine love?**

# WILLING TO LISTEN

A wise warning to someone who will listen
is as valuable as gold earrings or fine gold jewelry.
PROVERBS 25:12 NCV

Oh Lord, I stand in awe of your magnificence and grace.
What wisdom do I have to offer in your sight? Teach me your
ways, my God, and I will listen to them.

I desire to have a heart that values instruction and
learning—a heart that will receive a righteous rebuke
and wise advice. Help me to be someone who listens to
others well and not simply one who speaks without being
correctable. Thank you for your Word that is good for
instruction in righteousness. Fill me with understanding by
your Word and Spirit.

**What makes the ability to listen to sound instructions
and warnings so highly valued?**

# BETTER THAN LIFE

Because Your lovingkindness is better than life,
My lips will praise You.
PSALM 63:3 NASB

Oh God, you are so faithful to your promises. You have set your plans in stone and they will not be shaken. You will accomplish your Word and will establish your people in righteousness and everlasting life. Your promises are filled with wonder and unimaginable blessing, and I will hold onto them rather than chasing the temporary pleasures of this life.

The hope of your good news is far better than I know to hope. You are to be exalted, God, for the magnificence of the plans you have established since the beginning of creation. I praise and glorify the King of the universe who establishes his faithful promises and restores his beloved creation!

**What are some aspects of God's promises that amaze you?**

# WITHOUT REGRET

Godly grief produces a repentance that leads to salvation and brings no regret, but worldly grief produces death.

2 CORINTHIANS 7:10 NRSV

My Lord, I thank you for showing me my failures and trespasses, for helping me to see where I have come short of your intentions. You have given me opportunity to turn from these things. My hope and desire is that I would not disappoint you. I want to be pleasing to you that your will would be done through my efforts. Thank you for giving me your Holy Spirit that groans within me over the wickedness of my heart and of the wickedness of this age.

I ask that your Spirit moves me to grief and mourning over wickedness and that it motivates me to action. Help me to put aside disappointment over the things of this life I may be missing, so my hope is firmly placed on the day when you will reward the righteous and according to their work. In that day, with the help of your Spirit, I will rejoice.

**What regret comes from worldly grief as opposed to godly grief?**

# No More Boulders

"Build up, build up, prepare the road!
Remove the obstacles out of the way of my people."
ISAIAH 57:14 NIV

My Lord, I ask you to break down the things in my life that stand between me and completing the race I am running. The world provides many distractions that can easily entangle me, and the comforts of this life can derail my hope. Clear the path before me and give me the strength to overcome obstacles and the wisdom to avoid distractions.

Your wisdom teaches me to keep my focus settled fully on the finish line, on reaching the day of judgment in righteousness before you. The day of your coming and the day you finally establish the promised kingdom is the true focal point for all your work in the earth, so give me the strength of focus that matches your own so I also keep my eyes on that day and live according to this great and certain hope.

**What are some of the boulders that stand in your way, making it difficult to fully focus your attention on the Lord?**

# Seize My Heart

Let us pursue the things which make for peace
and the things by which one may edify another.
ROMANS 14:19 NKJV

My Lord, you have made it clear that we will face trouble
and difficulty in this life, but we can rest assured that your
rest and peace are coming. It is certain and will not be
overthrown, so empower me to pursue it and to prepare
myself for it. Fill me with wisdom and understanding so I
may encourage others and help to build them up in strength
and hope so we all run this race together.

Father, I look to you to spark my imagination and fill me
with wonder about the promises you have made. Give me a
clear picture of the majesty you will bring with you when you
come, and let it inspire devotion in me to press through the
most difficult trial. Magnify the wonder of your great name,
so my heart will align itself with yours. Fill me with joyful
assurance because of your faithfulness.

**What is the thing that God wants to grip your desire
and longing?**

# Too Much

"Come to me, all who labor and are heavy laden,
and I will give you rest."
MATTHEW 11:28 ESV

Thank you, oh great King, for offering me your hand of peace and fellowship and welcoming me to take part in your glorious kingdom. I am glad you have considered me and though my thoughts have always been so concerned for myself in life, you presented me with a chance to become something more than that. I am grateful that you desired to be reconciled with me and to extend mercy to me.

I see that you are a good provider and a strong protector. Your protection will shield me from the things that weigh me down and wear me out. I will follow your way of righteousness rather than my own poor understanding. I look forward to the rest you have in store for me. I will trust in you and make myself available to you for your will. You are my King and I give you honor.

**What can help you relieve the stress and burdens of your life?**

# SELF-DISCIPLINE

Since we are approaching the end of all things, be intentional,
purposeful, and self-controlled so that you can be given to prayer.
1 PETER 4:7 TPT

Father, when Jesus went to the garden before his
crucifixion, he told his disciples to stay alert and pray so
they would not fall into temptation because he knew that
a very difficult thing was about to happen. The night often
seems darkest just before the light begins to dawn. May
your Holy Spirit give me wisdom and understanding to
remain awake as the time of your arrival approaches. Teach
me the self-control that keeps me from being distracted by
worldly desires so I may continually seek your strengthening
and encouragement, without which I would not be able to
complete the task of growing in righteousness.

Strengthen my weak spots according to your Spirit so that
your power flows through me to sustain me in my greatest
need and help me deliver an appropriate testimony to
others. Thank you for sharing your desires and will with me
through your Spirit.

**How does self-control help you to be watchful as the
day of Jesus' return gets closer?**

# ACCOUNTABILITY

As iron sharpens iron,
so a friend sharpens a friend.
PROVERBS 27:17 NLT

Thank you for the fellowship of believers you have provided for me, Father. It is good to train together with others who also seek to enter your kingdom. Help me to comfort and support my brothers as we learn to live in righteousness. Give me grace to challenge and to receive instruction from others, for you have given us our friendships to be built up together into the image of Jesus.

May my interactions with others not be condemning or harsh so they are built up and do not feel attacked or shamed, driving them away from your goodness and mercy. Help me to bind up wounds rather than cause or amplify them, for your heart toward us is also good.

**How does friendly sharpening work out practically in your life?**

# TAKE COURAGE

He said, "Come." And when Peter had come down out of the boat,
he walked on the water to go to Jesus.
MATTHEW 14:29 NKJV

My Lord, I pray you strengthen me and encourage me. Fill me with trust concerning your sovereignty and faith that you are the restorer of the world. You will make me strong to withstand the greatest opposition and I will be able to overcome the hardest obstacles. Help me to train my eyes on the hope of your promises and the truth of your mighty works alone, and I will persevere in walking toward you.

I rely on your Spirit to fill me with wisdom and self-control to follow the path you have set before me and to run it with endurance. By your grace, I will not grow weary in doing good or be distracted by the temptations of the world.

**What are a couple of areas you could use strengthening in order to overcome?**

# No Despair

The righteous person may have many troubles,
but the LORD delivers him from them all.
PSALM 34:19 NIV

My Lord, you are my strong tower and I trust in you for deliverance and restoration. I know you will establish righteousness in the earth in your wisdom and timing, and I will not be ashamed because of my faith. I can endure many difficulties in this life in hopeful anticipation of your arrival because I know that you will fulfill all the promises you have made. You will give peace to your people and blessing will flow to the nations.

Thank you for teaching me and giving me understanding of your ways so I may stand steadfastly in the hope of your salvation. Your plans are fantastic and amazing in their genius and wisdom; I marvel at the intricacy with which you weave together your purposes in each action. Until the dawning of that day, grant me your peace and joy for your glory.

**Why do you think God delivers you from some troubles but not all?**

# BEYOND REASON

What should we say about this? If God is for us,
no one can defeat us.
ROMANS 8:31 NCV

My Lord, I ask for permission to stand in the assembly of the righteous. I pledge my allegiance to you, my King, and desire to be considered one of your ambassadors, spreading the good news of your return to all the people of the earth.

The nations war against your wise rule and they hate the message of peace you offer, and your ambassadors are attacked and abused because of your name. Even so, you will not let me be put to shame. You give me life everlasting. Strengthen me with this knowledge. Let it sink deep within my soul and I will be able to speak with conviction about you.

**What is the one thing that could overthrow the certainty of your participation in God's victory?**

# SURRENDERED

Instead, you ought to say, "If the Lord wills,
we will live and also do this or that."
JAMES 4:15 NCV

Father, I surrender my hopes and dreams to you and submit
to your sovereignty over the steps of my path. I know
that whatever you have ordained is right and true, and
whichever of my dreams are from you will be granted to
me. Let me learn from Abraham's example and not try to
step into the role of fulfilling my own vision, but, like David,
I desire to wait on you and wait for you to deliver me into
what you have promised.

I will trust in your wisdom and await the day of your decision.
I will live my life by your leave, understanding that if you
desire something different than the steps I take, I will submit
to them as you show me. Have your way in the life path I
take and straighten it before me in accordance with your
will.

**Have you ever sought to help God fulfill his promises?**

# LEAN IN CLOSER

He gives more grace. Therefore it says, "God opposes the proud, but gives grace to the humble."

JAMES 4:6 ESV

Father, I bow before you, the King of the whole universe. What am I that you would consider me? I choose to defer to you and your sovereignty and give up my own wisdom. I recognize and understand that the way I look at the world and the decisions I make are not in line with what is best, nor what you intend for the creation. I put aside my wisdom and put my hope and trust in you.

Lord, I ask for your good will. I pray that you will grant me a place in your kingdom though I have nothing of my own to offer to you. What you give I will receive, and I rejoice in your gracious mercy. Glorious God and King, be exalted in my heart; be exalted in all the earth.

**Why does God value and exalt humble people? What are some ways that your own heart remains proud toward God?**

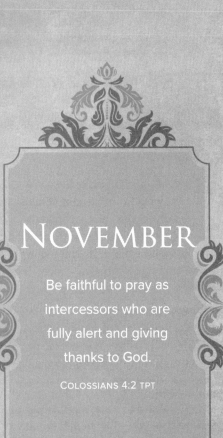

# November

Be faithful to pray as
intercessors who are
fully alert and giving
thanks to God.

Colossians 4:2 tpt

# There Is Hope

"You will have confidence, because there is hope;
you will be protected and take your rest in safety."
JOB 11:18 NRSV

Oh Lord, for those who place their hope in you, you have
promised great joy and relief from the troubles in this life.
Keep me in your good graces according to the work of your
Holy Spirit. Make me into the man you desired when you
established humanity's governorship on the earth.

May I act in compassion, mercy, and goodness to all and to
your good creation. I know that I will not be put to shame in
the day of reckoning, but that you will lift my head. May I
be found as a good and faithful servant in your eyes, my
King, and find refuge in the company of your people.
I have confidence in you, and I set my hope in your
righteous decrees.

**What is the hope God offers to those who will
accept it?**

# Pray for Others

Confess your sins to each other and pray for each other so that you may be healed. The earnest prayer of a righteous person has great power and produces wonderful results.

JAMES 5:16 NLT

Father, I ask that you help to maintain the unity of your body in their pursuit of you. Cause me to look out for my fellow servants and keep them in the forefront of my requests. Help me to stand in the gap for others in their weaknesses and to share my own weakness with others so we may stand together in the light of your joy.

Let no condemnation enter my heart for the struggles of my companions, nor pity, but give me true compassion to come alongside and give them courage to withstand the temptations we all face. Your ways of creating compassion and character in your people are so inexpressible in their beauty and effectiveness. May I truly submit to the lovingkindness you desire me to show others.

**Have you had a time when you did not feel supported in your struggles? What did you learn about how to be a friend to others?**

# UNTIL I DO

Certainly God has heard me;
He has attended to the voice of my prayer.
PSALM 66:19 NKJV

Hear my requests, oh God, for I need your great power
and strength. I rely on you and trust you for all provision;
please don't leave me in shame. Magnify your name in my
eyes as you sustain me and lift me. I am so grateful for your
goodness to me and that you have given me your attention.
Hear my pleas for help and fulfill your great Word.

Establish righteousness according to your wisdom. Restore
your people, healing the wounds and bringing life back to
the dead. Exalt your name among the nations as you fulfill
your faithfulness to your covenant people. Provide for my
needs. Create in me a righteous heart that is not false.
Thank you for your great mercy and for hearing me when
I call to you.

**Whose prayers does God pay attention to and fulfill?**

# Not Alone

The LORD God said, "It is not good for the man to be alone.
I will make a helper suitable for him."
GENESIS 2:18 NIV

Lord, you have seen my need for companionship. I thank you for the friends and family you have given me. The whole earth is filled with people because you desired a people made in your own image that could interact with you. You have made a way for us to increase and so we have. Thank you for providing so many different people with whom I may interact. Help me to see them. Help me to really connect with others and not simply pass them by.

Open my heart and my eyes to what they need, to what they are feeling. Give me your divine insight to see into their hearts and give me wisdom to know how to serve them and lift their spirits. May I be a blessing to others, and may they be a blessing to me. Help us to live in unity and peace.

**Who has God given you as a companion today?**

# GOLDEN RULE

"Do to others what you want them to do to you. This is the
meaning of the law of Moses and the teaching of the prophets."
MATTHEW 7:12 NCV

Father fill me with your compassion and empathy for all
people according to faith in your great promises. You have
promised to restore those who live with selflessness and
servant attitudes toward others, not seeking their own
exaltation at the expense of others. This is the heart of all
your desires for humanity on the earth.

Help me to live in accordance with this understanding,
believing that you will take care of my needs. I know I don't
need to take advantage of others to provide for myself.
You have freed me to love others with righteousness and
faithfulness. You have opened the way for your care and
compassion to go into the whole earth. May I fulfill your will
just as you have set it forth in the law and the prophets. Be
glorified in its fulfillment.

**Is the golden rule a new command from Jesus?**

# LET LOVE RULE

Beyond all these things put on love,
which is the perfect bond of unity.
COLOSSIANS 3:14 NASB

Lord, you are faithful to your people, not willing to lay them aside or put them away. You are diligent to fulfill your obligations in joy and generosity. Your faithfulness is the heart of love, for you willingly oblige yourself to your people and then you never go back on your oaths. Your faithfulness to your covenants of peace are at the heart of what brings stability in your kingdom, for if you did not love your people in this way, no one could stand before you.

You are caring and compassionate, merciful and gracious, and your faithfulness holds this all together giving us the ability to trust you and to truly give ourselves to you. Lord, I want to be like you to the rest of your people. May that be the defining characteristic of my relationships. I wish to faithfully love and support my brothers so we are all held together in our pursuit of the day of your righteousness.

**How is love the perfect bond of unity?**

# I Am Yours

"I have not come to call the righteous but sinners to repentance."
LUKE 5:32 ESV

When I consider my roots, God, and think from where I come, I am humbled and overjoyed about your benevolent offering of peace. You have not considered my heritage as something to disqualify me from your offer but have granted me a chance to be part of your family. Though I am nothing and my ways have been worldly and worthless to you, I turn from them and seek you.

Thank you for your mercy; thank you for your goodness; thank you for your compassion. May these not return to you empty but produce a harvest of people who willingly turn to you for their support and provision. Though corruption runs deep, you are not deterred in your efforts to change the minds of the wicked. For their sake, humble those who improperly think they are righteous. Lay low the arrogance of the proud. Be glorified in all the earth, God.

**What kind of person does God long to call his own?**

# GREATER GOOD

We know love by this, that he laid down his life for us—
and we ought to lay down our lives for one another.
1 JOHN 3:16 NRSV

Oh Lord, you have shown such great compassion in sending
your Son to die as a mere human. He experienced life
like the rest of us and like us, he didn't want to lose the
life you had given him. Yet even so, he willingly submitted
to crucifixion death to provide a substitution for the
punishment we deserve, so that you would offer us the
peace we do not deserve. He gave us the example of a life
dedicated to your service, God.

May I not love my life so much as to shrink back from
suffering on behalf of my brothers. Give me courage to stand
fast in the face of difficulty for the sake of your name and to
offer support to your people. I love life; I do not want to die,
but with your support and encouragement, I will sacrifice
what you have given me for the sake of my neighbor. Lord,
build in me this courage and strength so I may be prepared
to act in righteousness no matter what comes.

**How does God strengthen you to love others fully?**

# WHAT IF

"Don't be concerned about what to eat and what to drink.
Don't worry about such things."
LUKE 12:29 NLT

Great God and King, you have created all things and they
continue because you sustain them. You established the
system through which the earth produces and reproduces
food and water and have established the various cycles of
the seasons and years. You hold the very keys of the cosmic
order in your hands. How can I be afraid that you won't also
sustain me?

Father, my fear of death and suffering can so easily lead
me to follow the temptation to seek immediate gratification
from the world's offerings but strengthen my heart against
this fear so I may stand in it and overcome it. Jesus taught
that I should not fear anyone who could kill me but had no
power over me after that, but to fear the one who had the
power to consign me to everlasting destruction. Conversely,
I will honor the one who has the power to resurrect my
dead body and restore life to my bones. I will trust you for
provision, and I will trust you when I lack provision, because
you are the almighty King of the world.

**How do you respond in those times when you lack
what you need?**

# Just Decide

Remember to stay alert and hold firmly to all that you believe.
Be mighty and full of courage.

1 Corinthians 16:13 TPT

Set my eyes rightly on the day of your glory, majestic Lord. Focus my desires and will squarely on the time of restoration. Fix my heart firmly with anticipation of your promises. Keep me mindful of the fact that the works of the Holy Spirit that I see are intended as encouraging signs of the work you will fulfill in their appropriate day so that I will not become infatuated with them and turn to seek the signs more devoutly than the day.

You have given your Spirit, signs and wonders, miracles and prophecies, to strengthen my resolve and to help fill me with the courage I need to withstand the troubles of the world. They are a mighty and beautiful gift. Let nothing distract me or draw my attention to seek the fulfillment of this present day, but always cast my gaze to your future fulfillment of all righteousness.

**How do you become steadfast in your decisions so as not to waver?**

# LIFE OF BLESSINGS

"Because of your father's God, who helps you, because of the
Almighty, who blesses you with blessings of the skies above,
blessings of the deep springs below, blessings of
the breast and womb."

GENESIS 49:25 NIV

I am overjoyed with the blessings you have in store for me,
God, even though I am nothing but your humble servant. I
am descended from nations who rebelled against you and
joined your enemies in bringing wickedness to the earth, yet
you have been disposed to grant me peace and extend your
shelter of protection over me. You treat me as though I have
belonged to your family from the day I was conceived. You
love me and train me according to your wisdom so I may live
with you forever. You fill me with every good thing that can
result in righteousness in my character before you.

May your kingdom be established, God. May your blessings
flow to your children. Produce extravagant food and wealth
and beauty in the earth so the world will no longer suffer the
futility of drought and famine. Exalt your name, God, so it is
magnified in every tribe, tongue, and nation.

**How does God's provision in this life encourage you in
your faith walk?**

# You Remain

Jesus Christ is the same yesterday and today and forever.
HEBREWS 13:8 NASB

Oh Lord, you are steadfast and true; you do not change with the seasons or with the winds. Your message does not evolve with cultures or with human advancement. You have been the same from the day you created the heavens and the earth until today, and your faithfulness will continue forever. I can count on you because you don't change on a whim. Your promises are yes and amen, and they will never be turned back. Your promises of blessing will be fulfilled.

I want to be like you in your faithfulness; help me to reflect your steadfast character. May I turn to righteousness and not be hypocritical in my actions toward you. I want to be true to your rulership in my life, so set my heart firmly toward you. According to your steadfast love, deliver me from doubt and uncertainty in my heart that cause me to waver in my support for you and turn my attention to worthless things that might derail my walk before you. You are my steady and strong support, and I trust in you.

**How important is God's faithfulness to your walk of faith?**

# Let Them Choose

When the people of Israel heard about King Solomon's decision, they respected him very much. They saw he had wisdom from God to make the right decisions.

1 KINGS 3:28 NCV

Give me discernment to recognize and understand things that seem hidden, God. I need your insight and wisdom to live righteously before you and to serve others authentically without deception. Help me to make wise decisions according to your wisdom and understanding. You have made me a willful person so I can govern my areas of influence with genuine compassion and care, to know what actions need to be taken to truly fulfill your desires.

Help me not to make decisions merely according to the surface appearances of a situation but help me to discern the way to determine right courses of action. Train me to be a seeker of truth, God, who loves well and chooses rightly. I am glad to see you honored in my life. Teach me your righteous ways and lead me in wisdom.

**How do you learn from Jesus to stop judging by mere appearances and make right judgments?**

# OUT OF HIDING

Whoever conceals his transgressions will not prosper,
but he who confesses and forsakes them will obtain mercy.
PROVERBS 28:13 ESV

Father, I lay myself bare before you and hide nothing from you. As my designer and the one who put me together, you know me and what motivates me even better than I know myself. I own what I am before you and confess to you what you see. I won't try to deflect my actions to someone else or blame circumstances for what I have done. Your mercy and favor to me are enough to give me the strength to acknowledge my character and how I have corrupted who you have intended me to be.

Thank you for your offer of peace which gives me the strength to turn away from my attempts to preserve myself and exalt myself according to my own thoughts and desires. I confess and acknowledge the ways I have transgressed against your righteousness. You have not given commandments because you seek to condemn me. According to your Holy Spirit, change my mind and conform my will and desires to align with your heart. Thank you for giving me the chance to be redeemed in full.

**How does God's offer of peace draw you out of hiding?**

# FAMILY MATTERS

If someone does not know how to manage his own household,
how can he take care of God's church?
1 TIMOTHY 3:5 NRSV

Thank you for my family, Father, and for giving me such an opportunity to live in fellowship with others. The way you created us to reproduce after our own kind is remarkable and how we grow together in relationship with each other is fantastic. Lord, you have established these bonds to foster humility in us, to learn to seek what is good for each other and not simply selfish ambition. You have given us wisdom about how to discipline ourselves and to train our children in righteousness.

Help me to faithfully commit myself to learning from your Word. May I humbly submit to your wise instruction rather than act as if I know better. You have given me these relationships to help mold and shape my righteous character if I will submit to the process. You are so gracious in the way you have established to work out our salvation, bringing a means of joy even in the trials that come. Help me to embrace the challenge with commitment and to faithfully care for the family you have given me.

**How are your relationships with your family members?**

# CELEBRATE PERFECTION

"Why do you call me good?"
Jesus asked. "Only God is truly good."
MARK 10:18 NLT

God, I want to emulate you. I need your Holy Spirit in order to truly transform my ways and change my desires to conform with the good things you have established, to love faithfully as you have done, to show mercy diligently in your image, to give generously even to those who hate me. You are the righteous and true God of all creation. All others have only been pretenders who have sought to steal the devotion due to you. They have perverted your ways and corrupted the world so the whole world is motivated by selfish ambition and the desire to hoard power and wealth no matter who is harmed in the process.

Your ways are compassionate and filled with service to all for the benefit of others. The one who makes this their way will be given honor and the privilege of serving more. You give generously to the one who gives generously. May you be fully honored in your good actions and character. May I honor you by emulating you.

**What is the definition of goodness in God's dictionary?**

# FRIEND OF GOD

One who has unreliable friends soon comes to ruin,
but there is a friend who sticks closer than a brother.
PROVERBS 18:24 NIV

Lord, your wisdom fills all the earth and you have left nothing untouched. Thank you for providing a friend to me who has faced what all men face, who understands the temptations of this life, who has endured the deepest of trials, and has called to me and offered his support.

You have promised he will come once again and indeed he will not leave me without hope. He will not abandon your people in the time of trouble but will endure with them, encouraging them and restoring them in their hour of need. How good it is to be known as a friend of God and to be called according to his name. I will not be afraid in days of trial because I can trust in the faithfulness of my friend who sticks closer than even a brother.

**How have you been blessed to have God as your friend?**

# THANK YOU

Let us be thankful, because we have a kingdom
that cannot be shaken. We should worship God
in a way that pleases him with respect and fear.
HEBREWS 12:28 NCV

Mighty God, how I give you thanks for the many ways you
have sustained me. You have kept me going in times of
difficulty and testing, and you have not forsaken me. You
give me what I need at the right time, and you make your
ways known to me when I ask for your insight. You are the
ruler of all of creation, and nothing will thwart the plans you
have established.

You are coming soon with your reward, and you will restore
creation, freeing it from the wickedness and sin that you
have temporarily permitted to last. Thank you for not
abandoning me to the world. Thank you for lifting me up
even though I did not deserve it.

**What do you think it means that we have a kingdom
that cannot be shaken?**

# ALWAYS HOPE

The prayer of faith will save the sick, and the Lord will raise him
up. And if he has committed sins, he will be forgiven.

JAMES 5:15 NKJV

Oh Lord, I am amazed at the power that faith has to draw
each of us to you and to assure us of a hope beyond
imagining. It is such a simple thing you have asked of us:
merely to trust you and believe that you will diligently fulfill
your promises. Such a simple task and, yet, so powerful.
Such knowledge and belief can transform our lives, can
change our minds and our desires, can infuse courage in
fear and strengthen the weak who are ready to fall for the
temptations of the world.

Fill me ever fuller with this faith to trust in you. I believe, oh
Lord, help me with my unbelief. I ask of your Holy Spirit that
you fill me to overflowing with the joy and peace that the
world cannot understand. My hope shall ever be in you, oh
great King!

**Is the prayer of faith merely faith for the healing
of sickness?**

# DESERVED THANKS

Let every activity of your lives and every word that comes from your lips be drenched with the beauty of our Lord Jesus, the Anointed One. And bring your constant praise to God the Father because of what Christ has done for you!

COLOSSIANS 3:17 TPT

Father, fill me with greater understanding of the work of Jesus and the example he has set for righteous living. He lived before you in the way you have always desired a man to live: confident, self-controlled, just yet merciful, caring, compassionate, and able to encourage and instruct others. He was compassionate to the point of sacrifice, in accordance with your own character.

Thank you for the way you have magnified your name through the work of Jesus in the earth. You are a worthy King for the way you provide all things to your people. I exalt you for your goodness and love. May all people give you thanks.

**What quality of Jesus' life impresses you the most?**

# WHAT BETTER GIFT

The Spirit of the LORD will rest on Him,
The spirit of wisdom and understanding,
The spirit of counsel and strength,
The spirit of knowledge and the fear of the LORD.
ISAIAH 11:2 NASB

Thank you, Father, for giving me an example by which I may live. Jesus has shown me what it means to be a man according to the image you established in the beginning. You filled him with your hopes and your promises, and he set his hope firmly on the everlasting life you put before him. Because of the wisdom you gave him, he was able to point out worldliness and to call people to turn from wickedness. He recognized the times and was fully committed to the purpose you gave him. His eyes were fully set on the kingdom you promised him, and he forsook all else in this life even being willing to die on a cross.

How can I repay you, God, for this magnificent gift? Strengthen me to follow Jesus' example and sacrifice my own life in the way you set before me.

**How has God brought your understanding more in line with his wisdom?**

# In Kindness

"You gave me life and showed me kindness,
and in your providence watched over my spirit."
JOB 10:12 NIV

Oh God, my God, how marvelous and wonderful are your good gifts. I am forever indebted to you for you have granted me life and you provide sustenance for me. You are gracious in all your dealings with me. Your kindness extends to all the earth, for you have established your creation in your good will and according to your great wisdom.

Your creation is awesome in its complexity and the way that you have orchestrated it to work together to provide all that we need. You are to be exalted and praised. I magnify your name and stand in awe of your phenomenal works. Your kindness will be known in all the world.

**What are a couple of ways you can show God's kindness to other people today?**

# HUMILITY OF JESUS

He poured water into the basin, and began to wash the disciples' feet and to wipe them with the towel with which He was girded.

JOHN 13:5 NASB

God, I would say that you have turned the practice of authority on its head, but in truth, it is we who have corrupted the role of governance in the earth. The greatest is to be the servant of all, so you have set the example in the life of Jesus who bore the burdens of his people and lived out the servant heart you have called humanity to live.

You, oh Lord, are the greatest of servants and you deserve the highest of praise and honor. We are not to seek glory and honor for our own sakes but for the sake of blessing others, and we show how genuine that desire is through our willingness to die for others rather than preserve ourselves. I ask you to build up this desire within me and give me the strength to live in service to others.

**What is the source of Jesus' humility?**

# HAVE MERCY

Let us therefore approach the throne of grace with boldness, so that we may receive mercy and find grace to help in time of need.
HEBREWS 4:16 NRSV

My Lord and King, I come to you asking for grace to sustain me today, to help me to persist in doing good and in following the path you have set before me. I need your ever-present Spirit to assist me by giving me the will to press forward even amid difficulty and trial.

I know that you are kind and merciful to me in these times, and you have abundant support to give to those who call out to you. I thank you for your sustaining grace that strengthened Jesus even in the time of his greatest trouble and gave him the ability to defer to your will rather than his own. I ask you for this grace even now to keep me in my way.

**What are we intended to seek God's mercy for?**

# MADE NEW

Create in me a clean heart, O God,
and put a new and right spirit within me.
PSALM 51:10 NRSV

Father, through the work of your Holy Spirit, I ask you to change me and transform my will and desires to conform with you and the things you have established as righteous and good. You have created all things and you made them good in the beginning.

Renew me, oh Lord, and help me to seek after the things you have set forth to be desired and enjoyed. Do not leave me without a counselor but renew your Spirit in me. May it draw me down the path of righteousness to the day of cleansing and renewal. Be glorified in all of your ways, God; magnify your righteousness in the earth.

**Beside the point that God ought to be obeyed, what is the reason for renewing a right spirit in you? What purpose does that ultimately serve?**

# Miracle Enough

"Will you never believe in me unless
you see miraculous signs and wonders?"
JOHN 4:48 NLT

I exalt you, my King, for you have done marvelous things
in the earth and have shown your great power and the
irresistibility of your works. Though powers in the heavens
and kings on the earth seek to thwart you, they merely
reinforce your works. The testimony of your miraculous
wonders speaks forth from all parts of creation, and even
more so from the way you have righteously dealt with your
people.

No one will be able to excuse their unbelief, for you have
performed mighty deeds in all the earth. I believe your good
Word and trust in the certainty of your promises; strengthen
my devotion to you and show forth your power. It is only
through humility that people will be saved.

**What purpose do signs and wonders serve in
people's hearts?**

# A Way Home

All things are of God, who has reconciled us to Himself through Jesus Christ, and has given us the ministry of reconciliation.

2 CORINTHIANS 5:18 NKJV

Glorious God and Father, I exalt and magnify you for you have given a way for each of us to be found worthy of salvation. Thank you for the great gift you have given to us. How can we ever repay you for this good news you have extended to us? Even though it is impossible, I will give myself over to you and the work you have established for those who call on your name.

May I be a righteous witness of your goodness and faithful love to anyone I encounter. Open doors for me to declare your generous gift so others may find their way back to you and be reconciled to you. My heart is overwhelmed with the goodness of your mercy to me! I pray your will be fulfilled in the earth as you have planned.

**How do you explain reconciliation to people who don't know its meaning?**

# Not Feeling It

Diligent hands will rule,
but laziness ends in forced labor.
PROVERBS 12:24 NIV

Help me set my will firmly to accomplish the task you have set before me, Lord. You have called me to purify my ways and turn from corrupted things, so strengthen me in the power of your Spirit to persistently pursue a righteous life before your throne. Help me to discern the things in my life that need adjusting, those that need strengthening, and those that need abandoning.

Though you provide times of rest, let me not become complacent because of that rest but continue to train with diligence. Exalt your way before me and strengthen me to walk your path of righteousness, for that is your desire as shown in the everlasting life you gave Jesus. He did not tire in pursuing your will, nor did he become complacent regarding the path you set before him. May his example serve to inspire me.

**What helps motivate you to do what you must when you don't want to do it?**

# WAITING FOR ME

You need to persevere so that when you have done the will
of God, you will receive what he has promised.
HEBREWS 10:36 NIV

Look favorably on me and give me the strength to keep
running this race of faith, God. Propel me forward on this
path and give me endurance through your Holy Spirit to
finish victoriously, not having turned back to the ways of the
world and not having stumbled over the temptations that
attempt to draw me away. Lift me up when I do falter as I
repent and turn back to you. Look favorably on me to not
hold my faults against me.

Help me to faithfully complete my part in doing your will
and grant me the reward you have promised to those who
persevere—salvation. I look forward to seeing your face
waiting for me at the finish line and goal of my faith. I hope
in these things to the glory of your great name.

**What role does perseverance have in shaping
your life?**

# First and True

Don't set the affections of your heart on this world or in loving the
things of the world. The love of the Father and
the love of the world are incompatible.

1 JOHN 2:15 TPT

Father, it defies the imagination to consider what eternity
with you will be like because I am so used to what is
currently here. Your promises are magnificent, so much
better than the reality in which I live. It is difficult to put my
hope fully in that picture because it can seem so fantastical,
and so I am drawn back to being satisfied with this world.

This world is not what you had in mind when you created it;
it has been cursed and is broken in so many ways. To love it
is to love something you have not wanted. Fill me with your
Spirit, my God, so that my desires are aligned with yours
and I can love what you love. I desire to be wholly devoted
to you, and that includes caring about the plans you have
made and supporting the things you have declared. Help
me to remain true to you as my first love.

**At heart, what makes something a thing of the world?**

# DECEMBER

The LORD is close to
everyone who
prays to him,
to all who truly
pray to him.

PSALM 145:18 NCV

# MAKE ME WISE

How blessed is the man who finds wisdom
And the man who gains understanding.
PROVERBS 3:13 NASB

Lord, you have said that if I want to find wisdom, I should ask you. You give generously to those who desire your good gifts. Teach me so I may understand the way of your kingdom, that I may know the plans you have established in your righteous wisdom.

Give me wisdom to live appropriately in accord with your master plan; I desire to travel the path you have set. You have promised blessing to those who choose your path and persevere on it to the very end. I await your great reward and long to be found acceptable to you.

**What about wisdom leads to blessing?**

# EVER BRIGHTER

We all, with unveiled face, beholding as in a mirror the glory of the Lord, are being transformed into the same image from glory to glory, just as by the Spirit of the Lord.

2 CORINTHIANS 3:18 NKJV

Mighty God, refresh my heart and mold me into the character of Jesus. You created man in your image in the beginning, yet I was corrupted in my way. Transform my way before you. Through every experience I have, polish away the tarnish on my image so I may shine the light of your righteous goodness.

Make me more like you in all aspects of my life and present me in the day of your appearing as the man you had intended all along, fully exhibiting the image you intended me to bear. Then I will see your face and behold my God in peace and joy instead of fear of death. May you be exalted and honored in all the earth!

**How is God transforming you into the image of Christ? Consider how he goes about that work.**

# STRIVING

"Don't work for the food that spoils. Work for the food that stays
good always and gives eternal life. The Son of Man will give you
this food, because on him God the Father has put his power."
JOHN 6:27 NCV

Lord, you have promised to provide for all my needs. You
have said that you provide food for the creatures of the
earth and the birds of the air and will certainly do so for
me who is more valuable, so help me trust you to do that.
Lift my focus from the day-to-day needs and providing for
the things you have promised to give, and help me to aim
for attaining your good promises: food that never runs out,
health, and everlasting life.

Help me to focus on your will, to devote myself to working
toward the character and image you value. Give me the
strength and encouragement I need to change the depths
of my motivations and desires. I believe you have chosen to
exalt Jesus as your anointed King, and that all these good
promises will be accomplished.

**What kind of food do you find yourself working for?**

# At Your Word

It is by faith we understand that the whole world
was made by God's command so what we see
was made by something that cannot be seen.
HEBREWS 11:3 NCV

Father, your power and strength amaze me. I am drawn to
the faithfulness you exhibit and the loyalty you extend to
your people. Your character inspires the desire to do and be
the same in my own life. Your Word is true, and you do not
change it. You have established your righteous ways; you
have given your just commandments.

May I live accordingly in the strength of the Spirit you have
poured out on me. Magnify your name, oh Lord, according
to your greatness and the majesty of your throne. Exalt the
humble of the earth, as you have promised, and make the
world to know that nothing was created without you creating
it. You commanded and it was done. Help me to believe in
what I cannot see.

**How do you continue to believe that the world was
made by God's command despite the numerous ideas
presented by the world?**

# LEADING ME

Whether you turn to the right or to the left, your ears will hear a
voice behind you, saying, "This is the way; walk in it."

ISAIAH 30:21 NIV

Lead my steps, Father, and guide my paths so I can rest
assured that I have been aligned with you and need never
fear your wrath. I need your ever-present Spirit to show me
the way, or else my eyes may become distracted from the
prize you have set and go after things that are more readily
attained.

Lead my heart, Lord, and do not forsake me. You are the
King of all creation and I choose to follow you. Strengthen
me to persevere and not waver. I humble myself before you
and acknowledge my weakness; guide my steps. I long for
the day when you establish your righteousness, and I look
forward to being restored, a righteous man, wholesome in
all my ways and able to achieve the goals you have set
for me.

**Does God's leading ever bring you to difficult places of
trial and struggle?**

# Free to Serve

As God's loving servants, you should live in complete freedom,
but never use your freedom as a cover-up for evil.

1 Peter 2:16 TPT

Before I knew you, all I had was to preserve myself and to
seek what would comfort me. I was the only one who looked
after my interests, and I would do what I thought best to
make sure I was taken care of, regardless of how my actions
would affect others. But now, you have offered me your
hand of friendship and have pledged to be my provider. You
have shown me your desire to provide abundantly more
than I could ever imagine and have made me free to serve
and to consider others in righteousness.

I am no longer bound to seek satisfaction on my own; I
am no longer bound to my futile ways of providing for my
needs. I have as my sovereign Lord the great God and
Creator of the heavens and the earth; you have freed me
from slavery to selfish ambition. May my actions now reflect
your love and compassion for others as I trust
your provision.

**What is complete freedom?**

# INDESCRIBABLE GIFT

Thanks be to God for his indescribable gift!
2 Corinthians 9:15 nkjv

Father, you are my provider and the source of everything I need. Thank you for building a generous spirit in your people as we learn to follow you in your generosity. Help me to give willingly and joyfully to help support my brethren when they are in need, wherever they may be. I know that this is the best way to reflect my appreciation of your generosity, for you did not give to me for my own sake, but so I could learn how to care for others.

Your ways are amazing, Lord, for you make provision for some people's bodily needs while also providing an opportunity for others to build character. Your ways are always so amazingly multifaceted and marvelous. Your generosity and compassion to me are beyond my words to describe, and I sense I have not yet gained a full understanding of what you have done. I am glad to have been provided the opportunity to learn more of your wondrous ways.

**What is God's indescribable gift?**

# NO MORE SORROW

"He will wipe every tear from their eyes, and there will be
no more death or sorrow or crying or pain.
All these things are gone forever."
REVELATION 21:4 NLT

I am amazed at the wonder of your promised blessing,
my God. My patience wears thin in anticipation of your
coming and accomplishing the renewal of the earth,
making it as it had been in the beginning. Thank you
for your Holy Spirit who helps teach me patience and
perseverance to wait diligently for you, but he also leads
my heart to cry out to you to hasten your coming.

For the sake of your people, oh Lord, come quickly and
put an end to bloodshed and violence, to sorrow and
mourning, to unfulfilled needs and lost friends. Your mercy
to humanity is great, and your plans are accomplishing
for us a marvelous harvest of righteous life and life
everlasting. It is good to consider the comfort you will
give me in the day of your coming, the reunions and the
feasting, the dancing and the joy. Fix my focus firmly and
completely on the day of your coming so I am ready to
receive you when you come.

**How focused are you on the promise of God's
restoration?**

# Hypocrisy

"You hypocrite! First, take the wood out of your own eye. Then
you will see clearly to take the dust out of your friend's eye."
MATTHEW 7:5 NCV

Father, I ask you to plumb the depths of my heart and
motivations to root out and cleanse all the evil and selfish
things from there. Fully purify my motivations and my
desires so they conform to yours. Be my example in action
and spirit so my works align with your desired plans. May my
actions be without hypocrisy but genuinely flow from a heart
seeking to please you and trust in you.

Reveal to me where I inappropriately act in selfish ambition
and refocus my gaze upon the day of your glory. I desire
that your name be exalted in the earth and that your throne
be honored by all. My knee will bow to you and not seek to
thwart your plans for my own purposes. May the motivations
of my heart honestly align with my words in glorifying you.
Thank you for loving me as a son so I may be made whole
before you.

**How do you fight against your own personal
hypocrisy?**

# TAKE ME DEEPER

Let us stop going over the basic teachings about Christ again and again. Let us go on instead and become mature in our understanding. Surely we don't need to start again with the fundamental importance of repenting from evil deeds and placing our faith in God.

HEBREWS 6:1 NLT

My Lord and God, I ask you to teach me your ways and lead me in understanding. Show me the depth of your vision for the world. Help me to gain a grasp of the righteousness you desire, the acts of righteous people and how they interact with what you have designed for the restored creation. I know that you are the God who will restore all things.

Show me what a transformed mind produces in your kingdom. Teach me the depths of self-sacrifice and humble service in your economy. So much of the corruption of this life is a result of arrogance, self-preservation, and self-promotion. Infuse me with your goodness. Help me to live my life in anticipation of the day I will live with you forever.

**What do you think constitutes becoming mature in your understanding of Christ?**

# Not Slow

The Lord is not slow about His promise, as some count slowness,
but is patient toward you, not wishing for any to perish
but for all to come to repentance.

2 PETER 3:9 NASB

I am amazed at your great wisdom and insight into the
affairs of men, Lord. You see the injustice in the earth and
hate it more than anyone, yet still you wait. You see people's
arrogance and the way they flaunt themselves before you,
yet still you wait. You have shown patience for the behavior
of humanity greater than anyone could imagine, yet still
you wait.

Your love for your creation extends also to the people
you have created in your image. You have sacrificed the
wellbeing of the creation in order to create circumstances
that would cause many to turn from their arrogance, giving
extensive time to us all to give our allegiance to you so
you might restore us all together. Lord, though I long to see
your righteousness established and your justice prevail,
I am thankful to you for your patience that gave me an
opportunity to turn away from the world.

**What should be the nature of your activity in the world
in light of God's patient endurance?**

# PEACE ON EARTH

"Glory to God in the highest, and on earth peace
among those with whom he is pleased!"
LUKE 2:14 ESV

What is a life that pleases you, Father? How do I know what
you desire? You have described the actions of a righteous
man in the commandments of your law, yet many have
thought they obeyed them and were not satisfied. You have
set forth a mighty and shining example of what pleases you.
Jesus lived his life before you and was found pleasing to
you, and you testified to this pleasure you had for him. You
lifted him to the heavens and set him at your right hand.

Father, I ask you to teach me your ways in accordance
with the life of Jesus. According to faith in your promises,
strengthen my character and transform my will so I submit
to your will, the one true King of all creation. Let your peace
ring forth to all who love you. May the message of your
kind, patient endurance act as a solvent to soften
hardened hearts.

**If you will have trouble in this world, then what is the
peace on earth about which the angels sing?**

# PLAN TO PLEASE

The plans of the diligent lead surely to plenty,
But those of everyone who is hasty, surely to poverty.
PROVERBS 21:5 NKJV

Father, you have given your proverbs as wisdom to your people, to teach your righteous ways which also means the way you have created the world to work. The advice they provide can be useful for success in life even now. Your wisdom holds value for this life, but it is intended to teach wisdom and understanding for attaining everlasting life.

Help me to be diligent to pursue plans that lead to everlasting life. I will teach my heart to put away quick gratification, to stop looking for its satisfaction in this life, for the result of that plan is to be cast outside your precious kingdom. Strengthen me as you have desired to do and assist me in setting righteous plans, aligning my plans with your own. Thank you for teaching me wisdom; thank you for your manifold generosity to me.

**How often do you see people attain success in this life while ignoring much of the wisdom of God?**

# Doing My Thing

Each one of us has a body with many parts, and these parts all have different uses. In the same way, we are many, but in Christ we are all one body. Each one is a part of that body, and each part belongs to all the other parts.

ROMANS 12:4–5 NCV

Father, your creativity is awe-inspiring. When I look at your creation, so much of its beauty is found in its variety. Even the multitude of people in the world are all so different one from another despite their similarities. Thank you for making the world such a diverse place. You have invited me to be a part of your family and you produce in me unique talents and experiences. Thank you for including me.

Even though the part I may play is different than what you intend for others, let me be satisfied and break down my envious desires which can twist my understanding. Help me to realize your generosity even if I do not feel like I belong, or start to feel like others are more desired than I am. You have a place for all who will answer your invitation and come to you. I am blessed to be invited to share with so many the goodness of life everlasting.

**What is your part in the assembly of God's people?**

# HARDER TESTS

Do not be surprised at the fiery ordeal among you, which comes upon you for your testing, as though some strange thing were happening to you; but to the degree that you share the sufferings of Christ, keep on rejoicing, so that also at the revelation of His glory you may rejoice with exultation.

1 PETER 4:12–13 NASB

Father, not all the trials I face are like the ones Jesus faced, for he was without sin, so his trials were never deserved but wholly due to the world's hatred of you. Use all my struggles and trials to shape my character and make me more like Jesus in my demeanor. Protect my heart during those trials that aren't deserved. Keep my heart humble in those times since those are the hardest for me to remain calm in. I despise injustice and when I am the recipient, I am more likely to want to lash out and take up my own cause.

Remind me that it is a great honor to be counted worthy to suffer injustice like Jesus did, and that I can trust the reward you are bringing to those of us who endure. Thank you for considering me worthy to be molded as your son.

**Do you think you face trials, troubles, struggles, and suffering in this life because of a lack of faith?**

# Just that Much

Christ proved God's passionate love for us by dying in our place while we were still lost and ungodly!
ROMANS 5:8 TPT

I magnify your name, oh God, for the amazing gift you gave the world through Jesus' first coming. You showed him to be the Messiah of Israel because you raised him from the dead, but you sent him to the earth to reveal your righteous commitment to your creation by the way he served his fellow man, both your own people and the other nations that have rebelled against your good news.

The way you have sacrificed Jesus in order to work redemption for your people, reconciliation for your enemies, and a testimony against the wicked powers and principalities who are headed for destruction is beyond amazing. To top all of that off, you resurrected him to encourage us all that you have the power to accomplish the restoration you intend. Your plans cannot be thwarted, and your powerful might will accomplish all you have set your mind to do to bring renewal and righteousness in the earth.

**How else does God demonstrate his love for us?**

# BEFORE THIS MOMENT

For every matter there is a time and judgment,
Though the misery of man increases greatly.
ECCLESIASTES 8:6 NKJV

Lord, you have established your sovereign rule on the earth and your will goes forth to be done as you have decreed it. Though humanity corrupts its way, you use its works to purify your people and draw the oppressed and downtrodden to yourself. You warn your enemies and offer them terms of peace on condition of their allegiance. Your enemies have been unable to thwart the spread of your goodness to all the earth.

You are amazing in your ways. Even though for a time your people are subjugated before the arrogant of the earth, your justice will be accomplished in the appropriate time. Strengthen us, Lord, in patient endurance until the dawning of that day, and may your glory reign over all the kings of the earth.

**What makes you able to endure persecution and still seek good for the oppressor?**

# Slow Down

The wise see danger ahead and avoid it,
but fools keep going and get into trouble.
PROVERBS 27:12 NCV

Father, give me peace of mind and heart in this day. I so
often want to plunge ahead in life, anxious to keep active
and not be left behind. Frequently, I look for the next thing
to do, either to entertain me or to keep doing something.
Teach me, instead, to wait, to ponder, to meditate on
your Word.

Give me the grace to understand your great patience, and
how you have held back from accomplishing your plans
for thousands of years. You have perceived what needs to
happen in your great wisdom, and you do not rush ahead to
establish your plans but are patient with us. Help me to be
more like you, waiting and considering my steps.

**How has God's patience affected you?**

# Bold and Yielding

Going a little farther, he fell on the ground and prayed that,
if it were possible, the hour might pass from him. And he said,
"Abba, Father, all things are possible for you. Remove this cup
from me. Yet not what I will, but what you will."

MARK 14:35–36 ESV

Oh Lord, sometimes it feels as though I cannot handle the circumstances to which you have brought me. I do not want to go through the trouble that I will face; I want to hide away and not deal with the situation. However, I know that you can be trusted.

You have set forth your plans for good to be accomplished. Strengthen me, Lord! I will trust in your way and the path you have set before me, for I know that I face it to mold my character and to accomplish whatever other things you desire. I will trust in you and wait on you.

**Can you identify something in your life that you want to avoid but God seems to keep bringing you back to it?**

# CONDUIT OF COMFORT

That we may be able to comfort those who are in any trouble,
with the comfort with which we ourselves are comforted by God.
2 CORINTHIANS 1:4 NKJV

The joy of remembering your good promises and the way
you are working in my life to draw me down the path to
everlasting life is encouraging to my soul, Father. Teach me
to give that same joy to others: to encourage the weak, the
broken-hearted, and the oppressed that you have declared
there will be justice and peace.

Magnify your good news in me so the world will know, so
the powerful will tremble and the humble will rejoice. Assign
me this task and equip me to fulfill your mandate, that many
would be prepared to rejoice at the day of your coming.

**What comforts you in the troubled times you face?**

# FINISHING

"I know that You can do all things,
And that no purpose of Yours can be thwarted."
JOB 42:2 NASB

You are faithful, God, to complete the plans you establish. You will bring to fruition the promises you have made. I trust in you and put my hope in you. My faith is not blind, as some have called it, for the evidence of your steadfast faithfulness is seen everywhere. While nation after nation have faded into the past, and knowledge of them is found only through archaeology and historical writings, your people persist and have expanded.

Your very creation testifies to your faithfulness through the way it cycles day-by-day, month-by-month, year-by-year. You have established the earth in faithfulness and, even under a curse, the beauty and precision of its working magnifies your name. Complete your great promises, oh Lord, and restore us as you have declared from the beginning.

**What other evidence has God provided you of his faithfulness?**

# BLESSED WORDS

A time to tear, and a time to sew;
a time to keep silence, and a time to speak.
ECCLESIASTES 3:7 ESV

Fill me with wisdom, Father, concerning your message of hope so my mouth may speak truth to encourage your people. May the understanding that comes with your wisdom help me to know when to speak and when to be silent, just as Jesus knew before his accusers.

Though many words could be spoken, you have patiently waited to reveal yourself in full glory, God, so teach me also to be discerning of the times to declare the truth. May my words be few yet pack power and be effective to accomplish your will. You are righteous and glorious in your ways. Fill me with confidence to trust your ways.

**How do you discern the times to speak or to hold your peace?**

# CANNOT LOSE

In all these things we are more than conquerors through Him
who loved us. For I am persuaded that neither death nor life,
nor angels nor principalities nor powers, nor things present nor
things to come, nor height nor depth, nor any other created thing,
shall be able to separate us from the love of God which is
in Christ Jesus our Lord.

ROMANS 8:37–39 NKJV

Give generously to me, Father, from the riches and
abundance of the power of your Spirit, so I will be fully
equipped to face all the trials and difficulties this life
produces. I know I can never be shaken or moved when
I put my hope fully on you. I am confident that my faith
in the truth of your Word will preserve me against all
attacks of the enemy.

What can move me when my eyes are fully focused on the
finish line and the prize of a race well run? Nothing in this
life can shake me when I, in the power of your Spirit, devote
myself to righteousness according to the example of Jesus.
Thank you, great King, for the way you preserve me.

**How can you be assured of being victorious in your
race to the prize?**

# Extravagant Love

A child has been born to us; God has given a son to us.
He will be responsible for leading the people.
His name will be Wonderful Counselor, Powerful God,
Father Who Lives Forever, Prince of Peace.

ISAIAH 9:6 NCV

Father, you are incomparably awesome in your faithful love to your people. I magnify you and glorify you for your abundant mercy that you have poured out. You have miraculously sent a Savior into the world—the son of Israel, the son of David—to confirm your great kindness to Abraham and to validate your promise to restore the earth and bless all nations through your people.

How amazing! How wonderful are your works! They are beyond fully grasping. The way you have orchestrated your plan of salvation shows just how incomparable you are as God and King over all creation. Be exalted!

**How has God's extravagance been manifested in your own experience with him?**

# VULNERABLE

"Today in the town of David a Savior has been born to you;
he is the Messiah, the Lord."
LUKE 2:11 NIV

Father God, how comforting it can be to be called your son. With such confidence you entrusted Jesus to a human body and a human mother and father. You were unconcerned for his safety even though you knew many people would seek to harm him. Your confidence in your ability to fulfill your established promises allowed you to place your Son in the most vulnerable of situations.

Even when all his friends were scattered due to their fear of his pending crucifixion, you were unphased because you knew of your resurrection plans. God, grant me this same willingness to be vulnerable that is born out of confidence and faith in the certainty of your promises. You have counted the very sparrows and you care immensely about your creation, yet you are not anxious about our vulnerable position. Thank you for your steady confidence.

**What can you learn about God based on his willingness to put so many of his beloved followers in dangerous and vulnerable situations?**

# POWER INFUSED

I have saved these most important truths for last: Be supernaturally infused with strength through your life-union with the Lord Jesus. Stand victorious with the force of his explosive power flowing in and through you.

EPHESIANS 6:10 TPT

Father, you are my strength and my support, and I put my trust in you to help me stand strong against the attacks of the enemy that try to derail me. Daily teach me and give me insight into the things you are doing. With the power you have given through the Holy Spirit, help me to declare the hope of your good news with appropriate accompanying signs, drawing people to your offer of peace.

I am in your debt, Lord, for the forgiveness you have offered, and you are even more generous in aiding me in growing my faith and my godly character. Without sharing your Spirit with me, and the instruction you provide through your Word, I would be helpless against the world. Instead, I can stand with great confidence in you. Thank you for your goodness and mercy.

**What is the power of God intended to do in your life?**

# FRUITFUL AND FULFILLED

Be careful how you walk, not as unwise men but as wise, making the most of your time, because the days are evil.
EPHESIANS 5:15–16 NASB

God, give me wisdom from the Holy Spirit to discern the times I live in so I may dedicate myself to things that are worthy of my time and will be fruitful to building righteous character. May the understanding that comes from your good instruction help me to choose well and to put away worthless things.

You have given generously of your wise counsel to encourage and strengthen me to fight against the temptations of the world, and I am grateful for your assistance. You equip me well with potent weapons to use against distractions. I am humbled that you would take such an interest in me to empower me to walk this path of faith. May your exceptional patience and stamina work in me to accomplish this task so I may receive the reward you have promised.

**What does it mean to be fruitful with your time in the context of the good news?**

# PERFECT FATHER

"Can a woman forget the baby she nurses?
Can she feel no kindness for the child to which she gave birth?
Even if she could forget her children, I will not forget you."
ISAIAH 49:15 NCV

Father God, how wondrous is your lovingkindness and the care you show me! Why should you pay me attention, yet you have called me your own? I ask you to hold me tightly and do not let me go. Fill me with your Holy Spirit and train me as one of your own children, molding me into the type of man that you desire to reward with everlasting life.

I trust you with my life and wellbeing, and I give you my allegiance for now and forever. I thank you for giving me such an opportunity. I am humbled that the King of all creation has set his eyes on me and shown kindness to me in offering me restoration. You are good and right in all your ways, and I pray you will continue to draw me by your Spirit into the character of Jesus.

**What can you understand about God's character knowing that he takes interest in you?**

# INCREASED HUMILITY

Humble yourselves under the mighty power of God,
and at the right time he will lift you up in honor.
1 PETER 5:6 NLT

Father, you have made me to bear your image. At times,
I have let that go to my head and I have acted arrogantly
before you, seeking my own ways and desires as if they
were of real importance. You call me to humble myself
before you and submit myself once again to your precepts
and commands. According to your graciousness, you
have given me the opportunity to once again give you my
allegiance and let your knowledge and wisdom define what
is good and evil rather than doing so in my own wisdom.

Help me to continually place myself at your mercy as your
servant, and—in your timing—I will receive the gift you see
fit to give me. Assured of your goodness, I rest and put my
trust in you. Be exalted, my God and King!

**What is the missing ingredient that differentiates
exalting yourself and God exalting you?**

# I Praise You

"You have pain now; but I will see you again, and your hearts
will rejoice, and no one will take your joy from you."
JOHN 16:22 NRSV

I praise you and exalt your great name, Father, for your
promises are certain and your restoration is assured. You
have confirmed that, in this life, we will have much trouble
and we will long for the day of your visitation, but you will
appear, and you will bring righteousness and peace with you.

In that day, your children will rejoice in your presence
and the greatest party the world has ever seen will begin.
Majestic Lord, come quickly and soon, for we cannot bear
for much longer the increasing pain and turbulence of the
world. Make your name great in all the nations of the earth!

**What is the most exciting thing to you about
Jesus' return?**

# JOURNEY TOGETHER

The LORD will fulfill his purpose for me;
your steadfast love, O LORD, endures forever.
Do not forsake the work of your hands.
PSALM 138:8 ESV

Oh Lord my God, your majesty astounds me. Your works are wonderful. You have set the stars in the night sky and put the oceans in their basins. You have positioned the mountains in their places and established the nations of the earth. You perform the miraculous as if routine, and you rule with righteousness over it all.

I know you will fulfill the promises you have declared and establish the plans you have set. I pray you will grant me the blessing of wisdom so I will walk in a way that emulates my excitement in sharing eternity with you. Do not take your Holy Spirit from me but make me pliable in your hands. Mold me in your lovingkindness and help me to continue to walk this path of faith with you.

**What do you think God has for you to do in this life? What can you focus on in the coming year?**